SPIRITS IN THE MOUNTAIN

VERY, VERY DANGEROUS, FIND THE HEART, FIND THE TREASURE

By

William A. Johnson and
Michael R. Johnson

Spirits in the Mountain
P.O. Box 5636
Apache Junction, AZ 85278
web address:
www.spiritsinthemountain.com

SPIRITS IN THE MOUNTAIN

William A. Johnson and
Michael R. Johnson

ISBN Number: 978-1-60402-557-6

Dedications

To Helen M. Johnson and Walter J. Johnson, Sr. without our parents it would not be possible for us to write this book for many reasons.

To the rest of our family who supported our discoveries; especially our brother Walter J. Johnson, Jr. and his son Lars D. Johnson, who risked their lives to help bring our discoveries out in the open photographically. To the treasure hunters, their wives and children who died or suffered for the greed for gold, all around the world.

Disclaimer

Treasure hunting is not just a hobby, it is more like a sport which you must train your body. You must always have a game plan and carefully study the playing field. We warn anyone who reads this book not to search for the described locations due to extreme dangers that could be fatal and not to mention, it is illegal to mine or remove any artifacts from the Tonto National Forest. People who hike into the Superstition Mountain Wilderness areas need to have a good supply of water and your favorite trail mix, shelter from the elements and a cell phone. We also recommend seeking professional advice before entering any wilderness or mountain areas. Always let someone else have a copy of your map and itinerary. Let them know the time you hike in and approximate time of return. It is required to have a Tonto pass to enter the Tonto National Forest. There are also other permits available, etc.

TABLE OF PHOTOGRAPHS, MAPS AND DOCUMENTS

TABLE OF CONTENTS

Introduction

Jacob Waltz (The Lost Dutchman) in the late 1800s, was a man who spent a good portion of his life keeping a secret that would someday make his life an open book. After reading this book, we think you will become a new believer in the Lost Dutchman's Mine and then, question its name.

The Peralta Stone Tablets, discovered in 1949 by a family on vacation to Arizona from Oregon found them sticking out of the ground not far off the highway. Fake or Fable? After reading this book we are sure you will have the answer to that question and why they were made and for what purpose.

Adolph Ruth, did he wander off in the wilderness in 1931 and die naturally or was it murder? This book will have you believing Adolph Ruth was killed for his map or maps that would lead someone to the same area that we believe is the Lost Dutchman's Mine and the Peralta Stone Tablets hidden treasures.

This book may question your spiritual beliefs. At the end we hope you will have that answer as well. The numerous and dangerous trips Bill and Mike take into the Superstitions will definitely show you that they have plenty of spirit.

CHAPTER 1

THERE'S A REASON WHY YOU'RE HERE

This story begins on a small island off the coast of Massachusetts. As children our father would take us to the Good Harbor Beach to show us an old shipwreck. He would tell us stories about the treasure that washed onto the shore. Inevitably, the closer we came to the sunken ship the more treasure we would discover. Pennies, nickels, dimes seemed to appear before our eyes. Mike and I would eagerly pluck the coins from the sand, filling our pockets and our imaginations with the stories of old pirates and more sunken treasures just out of our reach. It wasn't until years later that we learned of our fathers "hole" in his pocket, and that treasure was his own, leading us down a path that would shape the rest of our lives.

That idea of treasure hunting led Mike to pursue antiques. He was a natural, and soon took me under his wing. It was in our antique store that we first learned of the Lost Dutchman's Mine while watching Unsolved Mysteries. From that moment on, the legend of the mine never wandered far from our imaginations. Like a magnet we were drawn to it, and 10 years later Mike and I found ourselves standing on the foothills of the Superstition

Mountains.

The Superstitions have a power, and it can be overbearing at times. It would have to wait until either we were ready, or the mine was ready for us to search for it. Soon our family would join us in Apache Junction, Arizona, and life moved on with its inevitable ups and downs. It was during one of these down periods that the mine decided it was time.

I was living out of my van, the weather was 113 degrees, and the Arizona sun was beating down on me with no mercy. I made it to the Apache Greyhound Dog Track to cool off and after one bet found myself up $130. I sat down and was soon joined by an old man, wiry, undernourished, and looking more like an old mesquite tree than a man. He introduced himself as John, and I offered him something to eat. I felt bad for him, and even though I was not in much better shape I figured he would like to get out of Apache Junction for awhile and offered to take him up to Canyon Lake for a much needed reprieve.

"God bless you." was his answer and good enough for me. We set off right after he was done with lunch.

Heading east on the Apache Trail towards Canyon Lake, John spoke up and asked me if I would like to visit an old friend that still hunted for treasure and lived up in the Goldfield Mountains. Paul was his name, and I was very interested in seeing him. After taking a right down an old dusty road we soon happened upon a man slumped over a steel water tank panning for gold. I could tell right away that he was a good, friendly man, and I was happy to meet him.

Paul was glad to see John, and he soon pulled up a couple of old folding chairs and the talk turned to treasure hunting. I was enthralled listening to these old-timers and their stories about the Lost Dutchman's Mine. I sat there for what seemed like hours as they talked about the mountains, and the treasure that lives deep within them. Paul could tell right away that I was more then just a local history buff, and before long the conversation turned to me, and what brought me to the area.

I told him my story, and how I was drawn to this area for reasons I still couldn't fathom. He agreed, and that for him the

Superstitions were a magnet, and no matter how far away he got, they always lured him back in. He knew I was down on my luck, and let me know that every night he would go down to Cobb's Restaurant at 7:30 p.m. if I ever wanted to join him. It was getting late and John was ready to go home. We packed up and I promised Paul that I would see him that night.

After taking John home I headed straight to Cobb's and Paul was already there waiting for me. We once again talked for hours and I could tell that he was a spiritual man. He offered a place to park my van for the night, and a bond was formed. A huge weight was lifted from my soul.

The next morning I was given a tour of his camp. Our conversations always turned to the spiritual nature of the mountains, and Paul was beginning to believe that I was sent to him by these forces. "Bill, I don't know why you have been brought to me, but there's a reason why you're here, and in time we will find out what that reason is," he told me one night.

Later that week Paul brought out a beat-up old leather briefcase. Inside were papers and photographs all pertaining to the lost treasure. He showed me some of the Peralta Stone Tablets. One was that of a heart, covered in various other markings, including six etched rectangles running across the heart in a diagonal pattern. The second tablet was showing a priest slumped with a cross and on an altar with the number 1847. Now I was beginning to understand what John and Paul had been discussing that first night, and that they just might know where the treasure was hidden.

Time went on, Paul and I had many spiritual talks over the subject and then one day he dropped the bombshell that changed my life forever. He felt that I was there to help him with a project, and when I asked he bent over the old stainless steel basin where most of our discussions took place.

"Bill, I've got a project that I have been working on in the Superstitions that I would like to tell you about and if you're interested, and if you want, maybe, you could work with me on this," he said to me.

"Paul, I'm already interested," I said.

Paul was starting to show some excitement, I could tell this was something he had been mulling over for quite some time and was anxious to let me in on it.

"I've uncovered a shaft in the mountains, about 35 feet straight down." His eyes brightened with every syllable. "At the bottom of the shaft is a tunnel that takes you further down another 75 feet. That opens up to a spiral staircase that heads down Another 150 feet, at the bottom of that staircase is supposed to be a doorway an old spiritual Apache Indian told me about. But you see the problem is that over the year's rainfall and debris has covered this doorway with about three to four tons of rock and dirt, and I need help to move it."

"What is supposed to be on the other side of that door?" I asked Paul.

"There is supposed to be over $91 million in gold bullion," Paul exclaimed. "I've had an archeologist examine the shaft and tunnel, and he claimed it was man-made and about 3,000 to 5,000 years old!"

I couldn't believe what I was hearing; of course I was going to help anyway I could with this project. Paul's combination of excitement, spirituality, and adventure was potent, and I was ready to start as soon as possible. He let me know that this was going to take some planning, and a team would need to be put together, but if I was willing to wait it out with him then I would be part of the project. I happily accepted.

I moved into a trailer on Paul's land. I needed to be close so I could learn everything possible about the Superstition Mountains, mining, and prospecting if I was going to go ahead with this new chapter in my life.

Several days later, Paul handed me a dusty, dog-eared book about the Lost Dutchman's Mine and other lost treasures of the Superstitions. Without any of the comforts of modern civilization, this book became my window into this enchanted land. Every word I devoured like a starving man. Late into the night, with the coyotes howling in the distance, and my 50 watt lamp with no shade, I would learn about the triumphs and heartbreak that had befallen prospectors before me. It was in the book that I stumbled upon a passage that stuck with me.

Find “where the turtle buries its eggs, and you will find the treasure.”

Something about this passage had relevance for me, and it wasn't until much later that I realized its full potential.

After a couple weeks of learning more about the mountains, Paul came to me wanting to get the crew together for the spiral staircase. "Three more men are what we need," he claimed. "Tonight let's go to Cobb's and find them."

That night we arrived at Cobb's. The air was electric, the heat wave of summer was over and people were happy to be outdoors enjoying each others company. I knew that we would find the three men needed for this adventure, and seeing the way Paul greeted me, I knew it would be soon. I was quickly introduced to Salvatore, an old Spanish prospector who had been working the Superstitions for years. He knew of the staircase and was eager to join us. Sitting with him was a cowboy named Mike and an old gold prospector currently working the Black Queen Gold mine named Fred. All three men expressed an interest in the work. We set a date for the near future and Paul and I returned to camp.

Something Salvatore had said in the diner struck me as odd. He knew I was an outsider, and had no business with the staircase, but instead of voicing any doubts, he looked at me and said, "I don't know why you're here, you don't fit in with us, but there must be a reason, and I'm sure we will all find out soon enough."

This is the same sentiment Paul had been expressing towards me for weeks. I began to feel that something was guiding me to the mountains and had a big plan in store.

That coming weekend we met at 6:00 a.m. Friday morning. Over several steaming cups of coffee we agreed to start the adventure. Piling into my van, the motley band of cowboys, prospectors and treasure seekers headed straight into the mountains and to the spiral staircase with no sign of trepidation. With the sun creeping over the mountains I had a feeling of calmness that seeped into every pore of my being. This must be what I was meant to do.

Upon arrival to the tunnel everything was in place. A wench

and ladder was still there from the last expedition untouched. Everyone agreed that I would stay up top, since I was larger then the other four, and they didn't want me to take any chances. Cave-ins are a real threat in this part of the country, and the last thing any of us needed was a big guy stuck in the tunnel with everyone else underneath them.

They descended into the tunnel and after 45 minutes I began to worry. Visions of mountain lions, rattlers, and cave-ins pervaded my every thought. Another 20 minutes past when I heard Fred call from the darkness. The first five gallon bucket was filled and I could haul it up. My concerns for the moment were unfounded and I happily winched up the bucket. From then on every ten minutes I hauled up a bucket and the day remained uneventful, albeit productive.

There was a strange occurrence around noon on the first day. From up top I heard some rumbling, and my first instinct was that there had been a cave-in. I called down and was immediately answered, so I knew they were still ok. After the day was complete I asked them about that noise. To them it sounded as if a train had run underneath them, and then they told me of the rumors of a large underground base built by the federal government in the mountains. To them the noise was just part of everyday life for a prospector in the Superstitions. They believed the government had a lot of projects we didn't know about and to worry about them was a waste of energy.

This work went on for several weekends. At one point a car began to show up and park near us. It was as if someone was watching our every move. We were never able to figure out the mystery of the car because soon afterwards the sky opened up and it rained for a week straight. All the work was for naught, everything had washed back into the tunnel.

Paul took it all in stride. "Every time I get a crew together something like this happens," he said. "It's time I get a job and make some money so I can try this again sometime soon."

Not long afterwards, Paul got a job driving a truck, I was asked to work with him, and I did. This didn't last long though; the mountain was soon calling me back.

The shaft that leads to the spiral staircase.

CHAPTER 2

A SPIRITUAL GUIDANCE

After several months of doing odd jobs and dreaming about the mountain, I grabbed my brother Mike and told him to hone his psychic powers, "we are headed to the mountains!"

Before we even made it to the door, Mike informed me that he was seeing large water stains on the side of the mountain. So we decided to chase that vision and track down the first mineral/water stains we come across. It was a beautiful December day, the weather was cool, the dust had settled and the sun framed the mountains. It wasn't long until we were near the foothills and Mike became excited.

"Look Bill, there's water stains on the side of the mountain!" he cried.

I saw it too, and started taking any dirt road that would bring me closer to that stain. With every turn down a dusty road I got more excited. I knew that the spirits were leading us to something important. We finally reached a dead end; out we crawled from the van with a cool breeze behind our backs. The desert was unusually calm, not even the steady drone from the nearby high-

The mineral deposit like water stain that Mike envisioned on our first drive to the Superstition Mountains.

way cluttered the atmosphere.

Mike looked up at the mountain and said “Bill, look at that head up there on the mountain.” That’s when I noticed the tortoise. The same tortoise that haunted my dreams just months prior in that old trailer in the Goldfield Mountains. The tortoise that held the key to the treasure of the Lost Dutchman's Mine, I just had to find where she buried her eggs.

Mike and I could barely contain our excitement. We agreed that this was no coincidence. We needed to do more research and let the spirits in the mountains guide us again. That night, with the desert sounds washing over the outskirts of town, we knew that we were part of something bigger than an old man's treasure.

The next day Mike went to the library to research the turtles place in the treasure. It was while reading *The Curse of the Lost Dutchman's Mine* that he noticed a treasure map with a set of directions signed by Don Miguel Peralta that was addressed to

Turtles head and flapper that Bill and Mike saw while parked at the foothills at the base of the mountain.

Jacob Waltz, the Lost Dutchman. Legend has it that he gave Jacob the map for saving his life. One phrase stood out, "Go to the south side of Tortoise Mountain, then go east."

Mike called me immediately, and we were soon at his house studying the map and preparing for our first hike into the mountains. Another map revealed a second flapper on the tortoise, Mike claimed to of seen this the other day, so we piled back into the van and headed to Tortoise Mountain. We saw the back flapper quickly and soon determined that the treasure must be somewhere near the back flapper and the head. We planned a hike for that coming weekend. It would be our first excursion into the Superstition Mountains, and we had no idea what they had in

Bill can't keep his eye off Tortoise Mountain.

store for us.

It was 6:00 a.m. the next day. Mike and I were anxious, sipping coffee and waiting for our brother Walter to pick us up. We had packed water, snacks, a cell phone, and walking sticks. He took us straight to a dead end, not far from the Tonto National Forest, and dropped us off. It wasn't long before we had reached the national park and felt we could breathe a little easier.

The hike was not easy, even near the beginning. Large rocks, jumping cactus and we had our own issues of health that made this extremely difficult. Mike had been diagnosed with diabetes, and recently had torn a ligament in his right knee. He was not willing to fail though, and I sometimes wondered if maybe this was a bad idea if I ever wanted to see my brother alive again.

Several minutes into the hike I brushed against a jumping cactus. It took several minutes and repeated tries to remove this ball of thorns off my arm. I was bleeding profusely and we hadn't

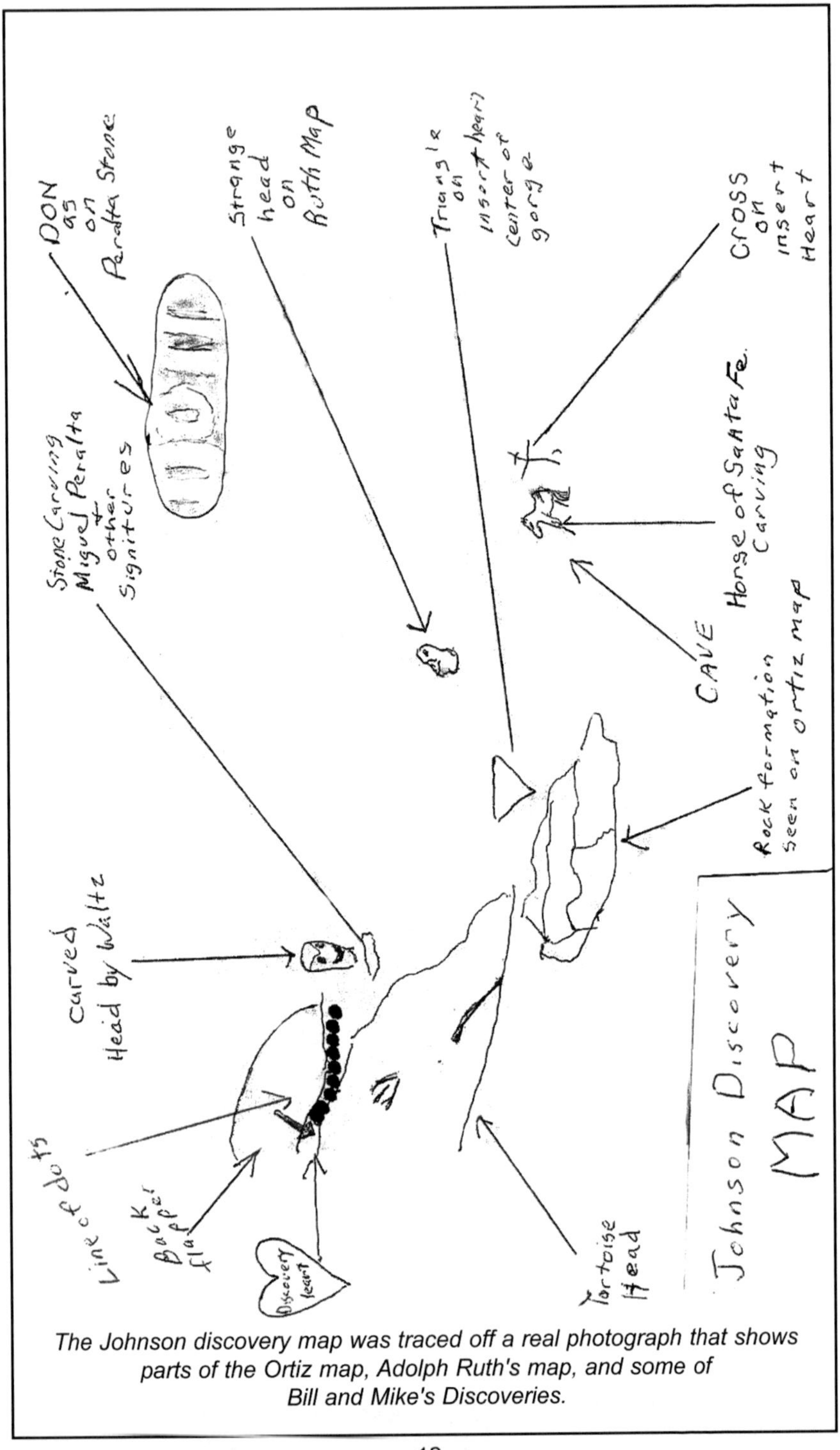

The Johnson discovery map was traced off a real photograph that shows parts of the Ortiz map, Adolph Ruth's map, and some of Bill and Mike's Discoveries.

Back flapper on the east side of Tortoise Mountain

even reached the difficult part of the mountain yet! The area had these cactus lined up nearly every two feet, the going was tricky, but persistence, a little luck and the knowledge we gained with every step got us through the early stages.

The mountain appears closer than it is, and after 25 minutes of hiking we finally reached the ascent. The terrain was tougher, and we had to stop for breaks more frequently. At one such rest we encountered a hive of angry bees; it seemed as if the mountain was doing everything in its power to prevent us from making the climb. Our water was half gone, and we hadn't even made it close to our destination. At this point we had entered a gorge. Huge boulders framed this wash, each the size of a car. Too much weight could cause them to tumble and easily crush us. The climb is getting steeper, the ground looser, and the dangers more real. Water is becoming a serious issue. We have already used over half of what we brought, and are nowhere near the point we set out to reach. Before us is a steep climb, and like most we discovered early that it is much easier to go up then down. On the top of this climb is another 15-20 foot cliff. If we make it up that cliff we're not sure if getting back down is an option.

If the loose boulders, 20 foot cliffs, loose gravel, and the possibility of not returning were not bad enough, the jumping cacti were more abundant and becoming quite the nuisance. At this point we decided it would be better to return while we still had water and all of our limbs. Covered in blood, dust, and needles from the local cacti, we headed back down the mountain.

After making it down the steep hill we found ourselves back in the gorge and sat down for a much needed break. Looking back we noticed a yellow square with mineral stains that inspired our imaginations we started to plan our second adventure back into the mountain.

In an hour we were back in our brother Walt's truck and heading home. Our bodies stained brown from the blood, sweat and dirt, water was all we could think about though. Water and the buried treasure that we knew we would be heading back for as soon as possible. That trip had taken us six hours. Six hours for two men not accustomed to the dangers of hiking in the desert mountains, the next time we would be more prepared.

Back at Walt's house I realized that the next time we should go back inside the gorge on the right-hand side across the head of the tortoise and inside the flapper. From that point we could photograph the area we believed held the treasure. After securing a disposable camera from a local store we set a date for the next adventure. February 2, 2006, the fifth anniversary of our beloved father's death was the expected date. This trip would be easier we agreed. The addition of a camera would allow us to photograph the yellow stained rock and give us something to study back at home.

With two more days to prepare, we hit the books for some research. Of the books we had, one showed some photographs of the Peralta Stone Tablets. On one of the tablets is a priest holding the cross and on the back of that tablet is the Horse of Santa Fe. Another was in the shape of a heart. A lot of people believe that they are a map of the largest and richest gold mine in the world.

For the last 57 years treasure hunters have been trying to solve the mystery of the tablets. Found in 1949, many old prospectors claim to know where the heart is. The Superstitions are full of heart shapes, and every claim that the heart they found is the key to the treasure has come up empty handed. Because of this a lot of people believe the Peralta Stone Tablets are a hoax, fabricated with modern tools in someone's garage. Until they are proven to be real, the mystery of the tablets remain.

Another interesting story from one of our books was that of Adolph Ruth. A meat inspector who worked for the government in the Washington D.C. area was given a treasure map by his son who was in Mexico. His son had received the map from the Peralta family and it showed directions to a gold mine in the Superstitions, near Apache Junction.

Adolph quit his job and began to search for the lost treasure. In California an unfortunate accident with a horse forced him to walk with a cane the rest of his life. He was later shot in the head while searching in the Superstitions, another victim of the Lost Dutchman's Mine.

They found his skull in December of 1931. His head in one place, and the body 1.5 miles away and a piece of his skull was missing from his right temple from the exit wound. Adolph claimed before his death, to of located the treasure. His last words from his journal were 'vini, vidi, vici,' translated from Latin it means: I came, I saw, I conquered. Scrawled on the bottom of that same page in pencil was "200 feet across from the cave." His story became an international phenomenon at the time. In some ways it remains just as fantastic today as it was then.

Jumping cactus surround the southern slopes of Tortoise Mountain.

CHAPTER 3

CONNECTING THE DOTS

The day before our next expedition into the mountains to take photographs began with a change of plans. Walt was going away on business, so only one of us was going to be able to make the trip. Mike, even with his health issues, volunteered. With no place to park the vehicle it was impossible for both of us to do it.

The next day we could barely contain our excitement. With plenty of water and snacks we headed to the beginning of the hike and I let Mike go. I had a bit of time before I could track Mike with the binoculars, so I headed back to his house for a bit. Upon seeing his wife, and letting her in on our plans for that day I was soon to discover that she had no idea he was going alone. After a long time trying to calm her down I headed back to the mountains to track my brother and hopefully be there for him if something bad happened.

I knew that this trip was far easier than the last one, but the desert can be even more dangerous when you let yourself believe that you have nothing to fear. Mike didn't have a cell phone this time, all we had going for us was me and some binoculars. I wasn't very keen on having my brother meet the same fate as the other treasure hunters searching for the Lost Dutchman's Mine.

After finally spotting him, I was able to relax a little. It had taken me over three hours to finally spot him! I was a nervous wreck, even though I knew the exact path he was on, and what time I should have expected to see him I was still worried that something had gone desperately wrong. It was a big relief to see him making his was back down the foothills. I knew he was safe now, so I took some time out to enjoy the scenery and imagine our life if we did discover the treasure.

Forty-five minutes later Mike was in the van and we were off. He looked a bit beat up, but not too worse for wear.

"So tell me about the trip." I anxiously inquired.

"I took a wrong turn through a very large wash," he explained. "In order to get back on the right path, I decided to climb straight up the alligator (this was a section of the mountain we determined early on looked like an alligator) which didn't look too hard to climb. Of course, what appears to be easy in the mountains always turns out to be very difficult. So what I thought would take 20 minutes, ended up being over an hour. Finally reaching the top I sat on the largest rock and pulled out my water and a tuna sandwich. As I was eating I noticed some scat (cat feces) near me. My mind began to wonder about the large cats that are known to inhabit the area, so I wrapped my sandwich back up and suppressed my appetite until I was safely back home. After getting back on my feet I turned to look at the large mouth of the alligator, after walking 20 feet closer I came upon a large cross. This cross was over 30 feet high, and since part of it was obviously man-made I snapped a quick photo."

The cross portrays the crack on the back of the insert heart as well as a few other markings.

"I then started to make my way around the eastern side of the alligator and came to a cave. I was curious enough to crouch down and crawl in a little bit. Near the rear of the cave was an opening in the ceiling. This I thought to myself would make a great place for a fire and to camp. The smoke would find its way out the opening and the shelter made a great combination. After finishing this examination I climbed the large rock that housed the cave. I knew this would be a perfect place to take some photos of the yellowish stains that we came for. From this vantage point I shot the rest of the film including the landscape around the yellow stains."

"After shooting my photos, I headed back down the path. I decided this would be a great time to search for some arrowheads and other artifacts. I saw an unusual shaped rock that looked more like bone. I pocketed it for later inspection."

We soon returned to Mike's house and after a long heart-felt talk with his wife, and many promises to never let him go up there alone again we were able to take the film to Walgreen's for development. With an hour to wait, we sat down and read the paper. Our nerves were on edge. We knew that if the camera was not too old, or the film not too messed up we would have some good pictures full of information. In the paper we discovered that a mountain lion had indeed been spotted recently in the area!

"I was just up there eating a tuna fish sandwich," Mike exclaimed.

"Mike," I said. "That lion would have waited for you to finish that sandwich, and then ripped your belly open to have his own bite, and take a little bit of you with him!"

At this point the developing was finished, and as a bonus for running over the 1-hour promise we were able to get a free 8"x10". We took the one with the yellow stains, the very stains that started this whole adventure and chapter in our life. Without wasting anymore time we headed straight to Mike's house.

Back at the house we were amazed by the quality of the pictures. We had 27 total. All of them were very interesting. On one of them was of the cross, maybe 40-50 feet high. It was on the right-hand side of the gorge on the western end of the mountain. We thought this end of the mountain looked like the alligator, so we always referred to it as that from then on. It was straight across from the tortoise head on the other side of the gorge. The second picture we found interesting was the one we were waiting to see, the yellow square with the black stripe-like mineral stains running down it. That photograph showed the side of the mountain between the inside of the tortoises back flapper and the head. The great thing about all these photos was that we could now study the surrounding area and look for particular markings around the yellow square.

The picture shows the yellow square with black striped mineral deposits running down over it.

With an old computer Mike salvaged from his work we were able to download the CD that came with our pictures. Not being any type of computer wizard we were eventually able to run a slideshow. It looked like a documentary of the expedition and we were very excited. Between the crackles, whirls and other various noises emitting from this dinosaur of electronics the trip came full circle, and we knew another one would be in the near future.

Later that night I was drawn back to the photo of the tortoises head and flapper. I was seeing something there. I noticed a line of dots leading to the yellow square. I remembered an old map from on of the books we were researching. Quickly scanning over that map I saw the same dots. Eight of them on the photo and the map, this was no accident. These holes appeared to be created by wind or something of that nature. This was the piece of real evidence that made us believe 100% that we were on the right track. I woke up Mike to share in this discovery. He was just as excited. After a couple cocktails celebrating how much a couple dots could get us so excited we started to plan the third trip for February 8th. Only two days away.

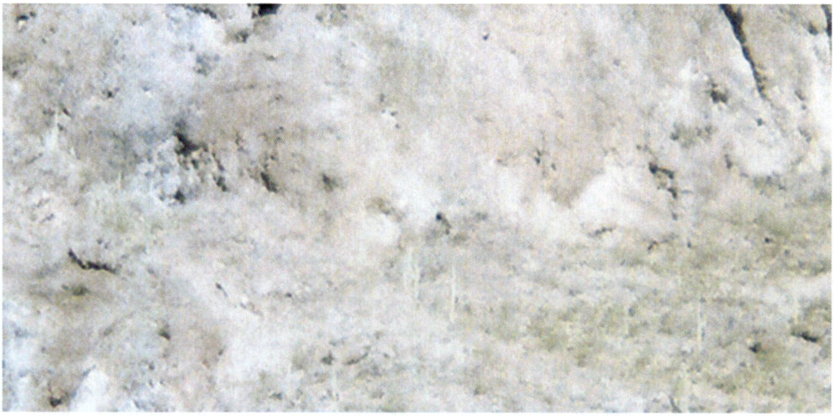

Line of dots that lead you in the direction of the yellow square just like in the Ortiz map.

CHAPTER 4

THE ALLEGED SKULL FRAGMENT

The next day Mike made another startling discovery, but this time it wasn't in any of the photographs, but instead involved one of the rocks he collected while up near the cave.

"Oh my God, Bill!" Mike yelled from the other room.

I came running; not knowing what could cause such excitement. Mike was standing there with one of the books and a rock he picked up on the last trip. He quickly opened the book to one of the pages that had a photo of Adolph Ruth's skull and the hole. He then placed the fragment in his hand next to the picture, and sure enough they lined up like a missing puzzle piece.

We were dumfounded. The chances of finding skull fragment that matched directly with the missing section from Ruth's skull were astronomical. We didn't know what this meant in the scheme of things, and needed some time to figure it out. Mike and I agreed that the next day he would take the piece to the Superstition Historical Society and talk with one of their experts on the matter.

The odd piece of material Mike picked up that resembled bone.

Luck would have it that the next day the president of the society was there. Mike asked him about the chances of finding the fragment. The man seemed a bit put off and explained to him that there was no way that anyone would find it because chances were it was shattered into multiple pieces from the bullet. He was also asked if there was any monetary value for finding something like that, and was assured that Ruth's missing skull fragment would be worth a fortune.

We cancelled our trip for the next day to look into this a bit more. Mike called back the president of the Historical Society and told him that he was the one he talked with yesterday about the skull fragment. He said he remembered Mike, and after being informed that we believe to have in our possession that very fragment the president, after a long pause, Mike told him we would bring it down to the museum so he could take a look at it.

We jumped in the van and headed straight there. Upon arriving we soon found out that the president had just left for a doctor's appointment. We were stunned since we had just talked to him, and couldn't believe someone that sounded that interested would just run off the second we told him we were on our way down. We asked if it was alright to wait for him there, and were given permission to. Several hours later we were approached by some of the staff and told he would not be back that day. It was at this point we realized the potential problems that we were going to be running up against when dealing with the biggest mystery in Arizona.

The next morning we called him again, he said he would wait for us and apologized about the previous day. We soon had the fragment in his hands next to a picture of the skull. The president seemed disinterested. He claimed to not know anything about the treasure, and told us that maybe it was bone, but there are a lot of bones up in those mountains, and that finding Ruth's fragment was not possible. I couldn't believe what I was hearing from him, the president in charge of the history of the Superstition Mountains was treating us and the fragment as a joke. We left in disgust, and soon began to ponder why we were treated in such a way. Do they not want to story to be told?

We then decided to take the fragment to the local newspaper. Kathy Hall, a reporter welcomed us and set an appointment for later that day.

Later in the afternoon we met her and she was very interested. After taking several photos of the bone, and of the picture of Ruth's skull she too believed that it may be a match. She would take it to her editor and let us know later if it was going to run in the next week's paper. She believed it would. Kathy promised to call us the minute she was given the go ahead.

We headed home very anxious. As soon as we stepped inside the house the phone was ringing and Kathy proudly informed us that the article would run. We turned around and headed back to the paper's offices to talk with Kathy and fill in any of the story she was not familiar with. We soon had the story wrapped up and ready for the presses, now we were back to waiting and hoping that no other newsworthy events would bump us from that edition.

The next trip was officially on hold until we found out what the reaction from the paper was going to be. The article was tremendous. Three quarters of a page with photographs so everyone could see how the pieces fit together. That evening I went to Cobb's for some coffee and tried to gauge the interest from other treasure hunters. There was general excitement about the story. Many believed that this was going to set off another gold rush. Everyone knew of Adolph's last words, and the cave. Was it a coincidence that we found the fragment near a cave? And that 200 feet across from that cave was the yellowish square with the mineral streaks?

February 20, 2006

'd Canyon News ☆ The Hometown Newspaper

75 Year-Old Mystery Solved?

Brothers find what they believe is missing piece of a famous skull

By Kathy L. Hall
The News

Adolf Ruth was a 78 year-old retired meat inspector and avid treasure hunter when, in June of 1931, he ventured into the Superstition Wilderness convinced he knew where a lost treasure was located.

He never returned and six months later, in December of the same year, his skull was found by a search party. The skull had two holes in it; a small one on his right temple and a large one on his left. A 75 year-old mystery was born that day. Was Adolf Ruth murdered for his information about the location of the Lost Dutchman Mine?

Two brothers, who wish to remain anonymous at this time, were working together on February 2, 2006, when on the way back down a trail, outside a small cave, one of the brothers looked down and spotted an interesting looking "rock". When the two got back home and really looked closely at their find, they realized it looked like the missing piece of a story with which they were very familiar. It appeared as if it might fit the hole in the skull of Adolf Ruth..

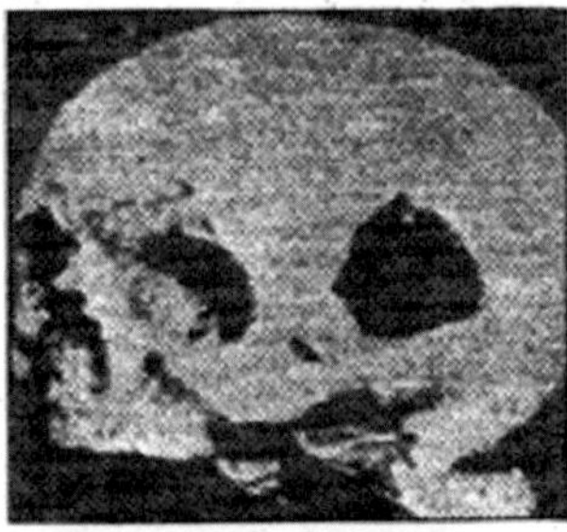

Adolph Ruth disappeared in June of 1931, but in December of the same year, his skull was found with the visible portion missing as well as a much smaller hole on the opposite side. Ruth was reputed to be carrying with him a map to the Peralta mines. Speculation as to the cause of his death has abounded ever since the discovery of his skull.

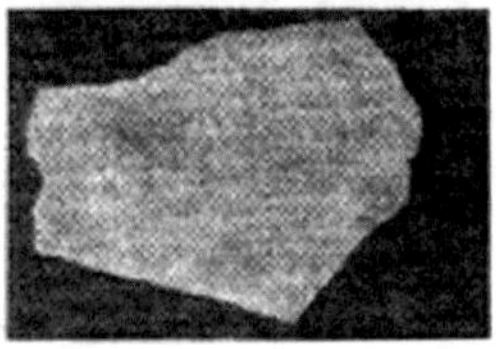

The fragment shown at left is what two local brothers think may be the missing piece of Adolf Ruth's skull.

There was been much speculation about every aspect of the Lost Dutchman Mine and the original Peralta Gold, especially after the death of Jacob Waltz, the Dutchman (actually a German) in 1891. Controversy has surrounded both Waltz and the Peralta Gold ever since.

Ruth was a treasure hunter who had been given a map dating back to the Mexican revolution, circa 1909-1923, which was reputed to show the way to some of the Peralta treasure. Two cowboys, who also had the prospecting bug, Leroy Purnell and Jack Keenan, packed Ruth into an area called Willow Springs on June 14, 1931 and by June 20 he was determined to be missing.

When his skull was found in 1931, it became national news and theories about his demise flew. Although both the Maricopa an Pinal County Sheriff's Offices con cluded Ruth died of natural cause there has continued to be thos who believe he was killed for hi information.

The brothers who recently found the fragment have a lot of work to do in order to have the fragment authenticated. They've made inquiries and learned that Ruth's skull was buried with the rest of his remains which were found about five miles from the skull in January 1932. The family of Adolph Ruth would need to be found and an order of exhumation authorized in order to match the fragment to Ruth.

At this point, they are excited and hopeful about the possibilities, but realize that their discovery may turn out to be something else. They have chosen to remain anonymous at this time because they are aware that no matter what the fragment turns out to be, they will be subject to speculation about their own veracity.

"We felt spiritually led to the site, as if his spirit (Ruth) has been wandering around out there, pieces of him scattered around. I want to prove he was an intelligent man and he was on the right track," said one of the brothers.

The siblings have spent time gathering information and enhancing photos on a computer and feel they are on the right track to being able to locate the Peralta Gold. However, their main concern at this time is to clear up their current mystery; whether they have indeed found the missing piece of Adolph Ruth's skull.

The next day, Mike and I were talking about how quickly this was all coming together. After so many years of this being a mystery why were we able to fit it all together? We are both very spiritual people, and we began to understand that this wasn't about us finding the treasure, that this was about breaking the curse of the mine. After so many years of death and sorrow we soon believed that we were meant to break the curse so the lost souls tangled into the story could finally rest in piece.

At this point many strange things began happening around us. On one of the photo's we took of the mountains from Mike's house we noticed a small glowing object on the left side. It was very small so we kicked on the computer to zoom in and enhance the object. What we soon discovered was that it looked to be a skull with the spinal cord still attached and it was staring out into the mountains. This was even stronger evidence that we were being guided.

Photo of skull with face and spinal cord attached.

We needed to find out more about the fragment. We had the feeling that everywhere we went would be full of denial and negativity. Regardless we set up an appointment with a lab technician at the Southwest Museum in Mesa, Arizona. The thought of learning if this was really bone was too undeniable of a feeling for us to let pass.

"You think if they tell us that it's not bone that we will believe them?" I asked Mike.

"Not really, it seems to me that the president of the Historical Society and the workers at the Southwest Museum are probably friends of some kind." He replied.

We soon found ourselves in the museum and being taken downstairs to the lab. The technician upon receiving the fragment instantly disregarded it as Ruth's missing piece.

"This isn't bone," he told us. "And here's how we can prove it."

He grabbed some kind of solution and an eye dropper. Putting a little bit on the skull it began to fizzle and bubble up. He let us know that this was just calcium, and even if it was bone that it was much older then 1931 because it had fossilized. We felt something was wrong, and asked him what the solution was, to which he informed us that it was a special type of acid that eats calcium.

On the way home after that we stumbled upon a great idea. We would get some solvent that cleans calcium, if this was really just calcium then the whole piece would be dissolved and we would have our answer.

We soon found ourselves sitting at Mike's kitchen table with a glass of the solvent; we dropped it in and watched it sizzle. Every minute or so we pulled it out and brushed it with a toothbrush to try prevent hurting the actual bone. After awhile it stopped fizzling all together and we were left with a piece we believed to be porous bone.

We soon called Kathy Hall again to let her know of our experiment and visit at the Southwest Museum. Feeling like we were running repeatedly into a stone wall we decided to take the fragment to the Pinal County Sheriff's department and have it logged as evidence. Kathy agreed to meet us there to document the event. The article appeared in the next week's newspaper.

March 27, 2006

'd Canyon News ☆ The Hometown Newspaper

Brothers Turn Over 'Skull' Fragment

Pinal County Sheriff's Office will determine if it is evidence

By Kathy L. Hall
The News

Two Apache Junction brothers, Michael and William Johnson, who had found what they believed to be the missing piece of a famous skull in February, have turned their find over to the Pinal County Sheriff's Office.

They felt the fragment looked like it would fit a hole in the skull of Adolf Ruth, who disappeared 1931 while searching for the Lost Dutchman Mine. The case got national coverage at the time, especially when his skull was found months later. The cause of Ruth's death has been subject of debate for decades.

The brothers have been unable to verify whether the piece was even bone and ultimately realized that turning it over the authorities was the best option. Sergeant R. Skedel of the Pinal County Sheriff's Office took potential evidence into custody on March 22, 2006 and a case number has been assigned. It is yet to be determined whether what the brothers found is the missing piece of Ruth's skull or even whether it is even human bone.

The story of the possible link to history was covered by *The News* on February 20, 2006, however at the time the brothers wished to remain anonymous and had not yet decided what their next step would be.

Pictured above: Sergeant Skedel of the Pinal County Sheriff's Office accepts "skull" fragment from Michael Johnson. Below, brothers Michael & William Johnson, who found the fragment while hiking in the Superstitions.

A few days after the article appeared more strange things began to happen to us. One morning while drinking our coffee we noticed a man walking his dog in front of the house. Passing our place he would stare at the house like he was looking for something. This wouldn't normally bother us, but he kept it up for several weeks, and was being dropped off by someone at the end of the block, and then retrieved later by yet another car. We knew that we were being watched, and that the article may be stirring up some unwanted attention. Every treasure hunter in the area knew of the last passage by Ruth about the treasure being 200 feet across from the cave. This new evidence had intensified their greed, and we knew that we needed to be more careful about this business.

We started planning for the third trip now.

CHAPTER 5

IN THE EYE OF THE TELESCOPE

March 4th, 2006 was the date we set for the next trip. It was a beautiful spring morning in the desert. The weather was perfect, and except for the pervading feeling of being watched every morning we were anxious to get going. The dog walker had changed our plans a bit. This time Mike was going to stay back with a telescope and keep an eye out for Walter and me. We felt that too many strange things had been going on for this to be more then a set of coincidences. We also had our cell phones this time, so Mike could warn us of anything suspicious.

He soon dropped us off at the start of the trail, and headed to a point where he could set up the telescope and keep an eye on us. We figured that we would be two miles from Mike when he could first see us. If he noticed anything out of the ordinary we would be just a phone call away. So far the coast was clear and our ascent into the mountain was moving along without any trouble other then the cacti and occasional rattler. The terrain was getting tough the more we climbed. Walter and I continued up the foothills on the south side of Tortoise Mountain. Suddenly the phone rang.

Mike was letting us know that we were now in range and at the moment everything was fine.

Gunmen to the right of the giant 'V'

Gunmen with rifle and a patch over his left eye.

Gunman with cigarette in his mouth.

There are large boulders on this mountain we have to climb over. As we climbed ever higher we approached a giant V shaped cliff in the center of a wash. We were around 200 feet from the tip of that 'V', and decided that would be our first resting place. The climb was tough, but after reaching the point our phone rang.

"I see someone else up there." Mike told us urgently.

Walt was not impressed and replied, "Oh Mike, they're probably just some hikers."

I took the phone from Walt. This was my third time on this trail and having never seen a hiker before I was more skeptical of Walter's theories then Mike's. "Are you sure there are people up here besides us?" I asked him.

"I'll tell you what," he replied. "Take off your red shirt and wave it around. That way I know I'm looking at you."

I handed the phone back to Walter and took my shirt off. Immediately I heard Mike screaming into the phone.

"You better get out of there!" He screamed. "Those other people aren't waving around red shirts, and it looks like they are carrying guns!"

We started back down the mountain. I had taken the camera out and was shooting pictures behind me, hoping to make the gunmen nervous, and maybe provide some evidence in case of the worse.

It's amazing how easy the tough terrain becomes when there are gunmen at your back. The cacti, boulders and thorny plants were brushed aside and whatever pain we may have felt from them was deadened by our adrenaline.

Meanwhile, Mike is having health issues. His left arm is going numb from the excitement of watching his brothers potentially get murdered. His blood pressure was sky rocketing and movement was becoming difficult. He does manage to make one last call, letting us know that the gunmen are still watching our movements through the wash and that we are not out of danger yet.

Finally we made it past the foothills and it seemed that we were safe. Mike called one last time to inform us that the gunmen had given up and were watching us from a distance. He told us that he would be there in 20 minutes to pick us up. Walter and I didn't feel out of danger, but we did have time to wonder who these strange gunmen were. Walter had worn his DEA hat. We also made it obvious that we were being watched from a distance. It appeared that both of these most likely slowed down the gunmen to some extent.

Soon we were back in the van and rolling straight home to wash off the dirt and blood, then get the film to the lab. Mike's arm remained numb. I couldn't stop shaking from the excitement. We needed to get that film developed and see what exactly we were up against.

As soon as the pictures were in our hands we could see them. They were everywhere, hidden in crevices, lined up along the cliffs and we even got one guy leaning against a boulder with his rifle and a patch over his eye and long gray hair in a ponytail.

We asked ourselves over and over, what were they doing? Guarding their goldmine? Maybe they had a methamphetamine lab? Or maybe they had read our article in the newspaper and knew we were on to something.

Walt was feeling pretty bad for doubting us. We all began to realize just how dangerous things could get with the infamous Superstition Mountains. Over 100 people have disappeared in the last century looking for the Lost Dutchman's Mine. We were determined to not be another statistic.

What did the Spirits in the Mountains want from us? To show us the curse is still alive and well? It seemed to us that we were being led there, and yet our lives were also at stake. We couldn't help feeling that we were being asked to help the spirits, and to release the curse. The truth will reveal itself eventually.

Later that evening Mike asked if I wanted my tarot cards read. He had been out by the shed earlier when he heard something fall. Opening the door he saw that it had been the cards. Another sign we both felt.

Mike set up the table and lit a candle. The first card turned was the heart with three swords. Suddenly the wind began to howl, and we ran outside to investigate. Gust of up to 50 m.p.h. whipped through the mountains. There was a big storm on the horizon. Mike and I headed back to the reading and soon interpreted the cards. Mike let

Snow blankets the Superstitions

me know that in three days the gunmen would be gone. Sure enough, three days later a snowstorm ripped through the mountains.

With snow on the Superstitions we knew the gunmen would be in danger. The Spirits were cleaning house, and clearing the way for our next trek into that enchanted land.

The fourth trip was now being planned. Walter even purchased a nice zoom lens for his camera with the thought that we could take tighter photos and capture more clues.

A couple weeks later Mike and I went to the grocery store to stock up on some essentials for the next trip. Soon after entering the store I noticed a man with a long gray ponytail and a patch over his eye! I motioned to Mike that this was one of the gunmen and we slowly edged closer to him. We got fairly close when he turned around and recognized us immediately. He began to shake uncontrollably and cover his face from us. He took off out of the store and we followed him. Outside he was screaming at his friend who was driving a red pickup. He was trying to escape from us and was very nervous. After several moments of trying to get into the truck, the door was finally unlocked and he drove off in a hurry before Mike and I could reach him. Later we heard that he had left town, most of the prospectors at Cobb's knew the man, and considered it good riddance to be done with him. Another obstacle had been removed.

CHAPTER 6

THE HEART OF THE MATTER

After a couple more days the snow had melted. With the new lens, we all were very anxious to get back onto the mountain and try it out. We were nervous about the gunmen still, so Mike decided to stay back with the telescope. This time we would head up high across the suspected location of the treasure where Mike had located the skull fragment and taken the photographs. Walter and I would go up about 2500 feet directly across from the yellow square and zoom in with the new lens.

Mike and I decided to check out the area from a distance before we set a date for the next trip. In no way did we want to run across people again, let alone people with guns! Grabbing the telescope we headed to the mountain so we could get a good look. Upon arriving we quickly set up the scope and immediately saw several yellow tents on the mountain. Not taking any chances we decided to take a couple more weeks before heading back.

After a couple of weeks we knew it was time to get backup there and take the photographs. March 17, St. Patrick's day and our mothers birthday seemed the logical choice and preparations were begun.

The day quickly approached and with sun shining and a cool breeze Walter and I found ourselves dropped off by Mike near the foothills and so began our fourth trek into the mountains. We were not going to make this a full day, a quick jaunt of two hours to the location would give us an hour to photograph and two hours for the return trip before darkness. This may have been a short trip, but it was very important. The angle from the location we were heading too, plus the new lens should give us a perfect shot at the yellow square and mineral stains. This could very well give us the lift we needed and put the incident with the gunmen behind us.

After an hour of hiking Walter and I had made good time and were 15 minutes from our target. Mike was making sure everything ahead of us was clear, and so far so good. A quick clamor up a steep slope found us in range and ready to shoot. Walter used an entire roll, taking pictures of just the surrounding area. He used another roll on the target, and before long our mission was accomplished and we were heading back down the mountain.

Within minutes of Mike picking us up we were at the Walgreens for the development. That one hour seemed forever, we knew that more discoveries were close at hand. Soon we had the pictures and CD and were downloading them onto our antiquated computer. A swift kick got the computer humming and the slide show was about to begin.

This is always a long consuming process. Carefully examining each photograph our suspicions were quickly realized when our target revealed a startling image. Zooming in on the yellow square we were stunned by our discovery, a heart, just like on the Peralta Stone Map! This heart was easily 80 feet tall, and did not seem natural at all. The yellow square with mineral stains was in the upper left wing of the heart. Looking closer we could see numbers and letters. The Peralta Stone map with the heart as a bull's eye also had a series of dots leading to it. Here we had the same number of dots with the wind holes, and a visible heart, things were coming together fast and was not a coincidence anymore. This was becoming very real.

We wondered aloud why this was happening to us. Our mun-

The discovery heart represents what most treasure hunters seek (The bull's-eye)

Front of insert heart

dane lives were taking a drastic turn and we felt that holding on to enjoy it was the best we could do. There was no stopping us in this quest to solve one of the greatest mysteries of all time. We printed three copies of the heart so each of us could study it closer with a magnifying glass. We were looking for any other markings that are also carved into the Peralta Stone maps. In one of the books about the treasure we found a full color photograph of the stone that so many people believed a hoax over the years. One of the first things we noticed were six etched rectangles lined up in a row near the upper right-hand corner of the heart. They appeared to read "DON". To the right of that is another smaller heart. The photograph we had of the heart had a lot of markings too, many of which were beginning to wear down from the harsh conditions. The mineral deposits ran down the entire left side, just as Mike had envisioned so many months ago on our first trip.

The more we looked at the heart the more discoveries appeared. We found the number 1847, and believe it to be a date. The 4 and 7 might be separated by a symbol, many believe that numbering an area like this represents a mine or mine shaft that has been sealed.

If you look closely, you can see the image of DON with a little heart after his name on the Discovery Heart.

The stone tablet that spells DON with a heart to the upper right.

The Heart Trail Map Stone Tablet

The Trail Map Stone Tablet with heart trail and front of the insert heart make a complete map.

The image of 184}7 appears next to the discovery heart.

As days go by Mike and I keep finding more evidence that's becoming harder to refute. The mystery of the Peralta Stone Tablets may no longer be so mysterious, if not down right solved. We cannot put the pictures down. This is the discovery of a lifetime and the adrenaline is coursing through us.

Soon Mike located something major in the photograph. About 30 feet to the right of the heart he noticed a white stone inside of a crevice. It was hard to locate, but it was there partially hidden by a shadow. Soon I was able to recognize what he was showing me, it was the priest from the stone tablets. This was not a natural occurrence, it had to be man-made. Knowing how easily the shapes and crevices in the rocks can fool you we also knew that this was no trick of the light, this was the real deal.

The priest is carved into a cliff a short distance to the right of the discovery heart. The arrow points to the pointed hat and the Priest's bluish face, facing into the crevice.

The Priest Stone Tablet

Mike and I were sitting back talking about this important find when it dawned on me that the whole gorge might be in the shape of the heart. I believed this to be true because of the V shape inside the gorge Walter and I were standing on when the gunmen had surrounded us. It was made of limestone and 20 feet high and 40 feet across. In one of the books we had been studying there was a drawing showing the heart and a V shape below the center. I grabbed the binoculars and headed straight to the gorge. It was a short drive and worth it, within minutes I was able to locate the V shape and heart. Yet another mystery solved, Mike and I stood there in disbelief.

The legend says that no white man will ever live to tell about finding the gold. We have Blackfoot Indian descendants in our family and maybe this is what's allowing us to make the discovery. One thing is sure though, a spirit is guiding us.

We decide it's time for another card reading. Every time we have one the wind picks up, the house shakes and the windows rattle. It can be quite unnerving. We feel the presence of the spirits and souls that are waiting for us to rescue them from the endless roaming they have endured. We were no longer interested in the gold, but with the power that surrounds this treasure and the death that has followed it. These spirits will keep us alive and on track as long as we remain true.

Our intention was to end the curse of the Lost Dutchman Gold Mine.

CHAPTER 7

THE ARCHING LADY

Mike and I started planning our fifth trip into the mountains. Our plan was to get in as far and close to the heart as possible. This trip was going to be twice as long as any of the others. The terrain would be far worse, twice as steep and an infinite number of jumping cacti. These were the known obstacles, only God knows what others might betray us. This time I would stay back with the telescope while Mike and Walter made the trip. The date we set was April 2, 2006.

The morning of the hike was upon us and with backpacks bulging with water we were ready to make the trip. The potential for more gunmen are real. We also feel that we could be watched. Our object is to not appear obvious and head straight to the heart so we can dig around, instead we are going to act like hikers and take pictures randomly near the area.

After dropping my brothers off I headed to the water towers to watch them with the telescope. I would need to wait until they reached a certain elevation before I could see them. With the sun beating down on me I surveyed the area anticipating anything. So far all was clear, just hundreds of cacti and lost of rocks. Finally I spotted them working their way up the middle of the gorge and getting ready to head up a very steep cliff to an area none of us had been before.

The words of Don Miguel Peralta never rang truer, "I go eighteen places, very, very dangerous. Find the heart."

Not much had changed over the years, and one of the reasons we believed to be right was the danger involved.

There was also another big concern about this dangerous trip. Mike has high blood pressure coupled with diabetes. Too much distress can be life threatening on the trail. He also has the bad knee which needs to be operated on to repair the torn ligament. He ignores the pain for what we believe in. He is now four hours into the trip and I know that the pressure must be unbearable for him. I see them stop for a rest and call with my cell phone to see how they are doing.

"Okay, Mike is breathing heavy but insists on continuing," Walter answers breathlessly.

They started back up the mountain and called to let me know how unbelievable the jumping cacti were getting. They were so thick that moving forward was becoming near impossible. They were heading west back toward Tortoise Mountain where the head of the tortoise was as well as the flapper. It had now been over five hours and they only had one more hour to accomplish our goal before they would need to head back down. It was high noon and there was no way they should remain in the mountains after dark trying to find their way down without being able to see where they stepped.

Finally they made it as far as they could go. Mike thought that maybe some mining had been done here before because of all the broken rocks. Walter took out his camera with the high powered lens and began shooting everything in the area, concentrating on the crevice with the priest holding the cross down to the white/gray colored stone with the hole. After using up all the film I got a call from Walter explaining that they were heading back, low on water, and unsure which path to take. The way up was extremely steep and hard enough going hands first. Descending was another story, not knowing where to put their feet it would be easy to slip and fall.

So they needed to find another way down, and this was getting dangerous because time was becoming a real issue and we had no idea how long the new path would take. They may have to spend the night there, and being low on water this was becoming very serious.

Walter called and let me know they had found another longer way. It would cost them valuable time, but at the moment it seemed the safest. I knew that I was probably going to have to meet them in the mountains with water. I was working on a plan to meet them when I got the call.

"I don't think were going to make it, Mike!" Walter told me with panic gripping his voice. "We are out of water and can't find a way down."

"I'm coming." I told them, trying to sound like the voice of reason. I knew that desperation had gripped them and they needed to calm down or it was going to get worse.

Soon the phone rang again, it was Walter completely frozen with fear. They had stumbled upon a rattlesnake that they still couldn't locate, but the rattle was close and they knew it. He finally spotted a monster snake, coiled and ready to strike less then two feet away, this was getting to be too much for the dehydrated explorers and I knew I needed to get there soon. Luckily Walter was able to hop quickly away from the snake and get out of striking range.

They were now about an hour from the giant V in the center of the gorge. I was still an hour and a half from them as I plodded through the foothills. Nightfall was fast approaching.

The phone rang again. Walter was vomiting uncontrollably and Mike was having a hard time breathing and his knee almost locked up with pain. Overhead the vultures were circling, and I was thinking that this was starting to look like an old western and not the great spiritual triumph we had envisioned days before.

I finally was able to spot them near the gorge, we were still another 20 minutes apart, but I could tell that they gained inspiration by the sight of me and before too long we were together and I was busy handing out the water. They gorged on it, vomiting every drink they took. They were both loaded with cacti. Mike would of dropped to his knees and laid there the whole night if his knee wasn't in so much pain. I gathered my brothers up and we headed back towards the truck. It was going to take twice the time getting there, but at least they might make it out alive. The chances of them recovering quickly were out of the question, I wondered if I should take them straight to the hospital for an IV to help the hydration process, but they insisted that home and lots of water was all they needed.

The sun was setting as we reached the truck; I quickly took them home and then the film to the photo lab. Afterwards I sat with my brothers and discussed the twelve-hour ordeal in the mountains. We had no idea that it could be so unforgiving, but we also now knew what we were up against and would be better prepared the next time. I hoped the photos would show us new evidence and that the trip wasn't a waste of time.

The next day I picked up the photos and met back up with Walter and Mike. They had both experienced a night of horribly painful leg cramps and were just now getting over them. The photos were a success, we were seeing lots of unexplainable artifacts, like a rifle with a long barrel leaning on a rock, and an old cup tipped over with gold nuggets spilled out of it. We had no idea if these were real or tricks of light. But it was the crevice that had the priest that really got our attention. From a different angle we could see a lady carved out of the rock. She was reaching out to the white rock with the hole in it. This was the type of evidence we wanted to see from the trip. Our excitement was uncontrollable, and all the pain involved was worth this payoff.

The lady figure was a huge piece of the missing puzzle, this was the type of figure associated with the Church of the Holy Faith; they call her the Arching Lady. We soon realized that she was inside a giant arch.

The Arching Lady with her 3D-effect can not be seen close up, it's just a flat wall. She can only be seen by photograph or by standing at a certain distance. The Priest and the Arching Lady are side by side pointing in the same specific location but they only can be seen one at a time.

Carved turtle to upper right of the Arching Lady.

This is the picture we hope proves Linda Peralta's claims of her descendants. The same Peraltas talked about in this book. In this picture is Don Miguel Peralta is displayed in his Spanish-like armor. Carefully carved signatures, with Miguel's proudly shown in the front. Other markings appear consistent with the Peralta stones with other family members portraits'. Linda Peralta lives somewhere in California till this day trying to link the Superstition Mountains to her family.

Now we pondered what might be in that hole. There was no way anyone would spend so much time carving this lady on the side of a cliff if the hole was empty. There had to be something of real importance there. We had to find out what that lady represented. It was going to take some research, but with the way the spirits had been guiding us we knew the answer would come sooner than later.

We decided to take the photo back to the lab and have an 8" x 10" copy made of it and then use the stores equipment to zoom in on the hole. It took the lady at the lab about ten minutes to produce the copy, and it came out wonderful. The hole was now about the size of my thumb, and with some zooming it appeared that light was shining from there, like something was reflecting. The hole was about 30 feet high off the side of the cliff, and we knew we needed to get back up there and see what was going on. If this was done by the Peralta family then there had to be a way in there. They either came down from the top using ropes, or from the bottom somehow. We had plenty of photographs to study the whole side of the cliff and come up with a plan.

For a couple of days after checking out the situation it looked way too dangerous for the two of us to make an attempt to reach the hole, because of our size; we are both well over 200 pounds. We started thinking that we needed a thin person who is not afraid of heights, someone who is used to climbing around on roof tops like a carpenter who is in great physical shape. We knew that we wouldn't have too much trouble finding that person because it's the adventure that we're on that doesn't come along everyday and doesn't happen to the average person but maybe once in a lifetime. We thought if someone had the chance to find gold they would jump at the chance. We thought about it for a while and decided to try to keep it in the family. When we mentioned it to our brother, Walter, he said, "What about my son, Lars, who lives in New Hampshire. He's a carpenter and he's in good shape and always climbing around on roof tops framing commercial buildings." We all agreed that was a great idea. Walter had a talk with Lars and just as we expected he was very excited. He said he would love to come out here and go on an adventure with his uncles, as Walter had been keeping Lars up to date on the happenings in Arizona that his uncles had gotten into. Lars was all hyped up about it and couldn't believe that he was going to make this trip into the mountains.

So Lars made his reservations for United Airlines for the coming Friday. It was only three days away. Mike and I quickly planned a trip into the mountains for the coming Sunday, which was two days after Lars arrives. Mike and I both agreed that if anything financial ever came to us out of this discovery that we could give him some kind of a reward for his helping hand. There is never a guarantee especially on something like this. After all, we haven't seen any treasure as of yet. Who knows what or where this will lead. Only God knows and all the spirits that are involved in this matter. All we know is that my brother and I started something that we can't stop until it is finished.

Mike and I decided that we will all go into the mountains instead of one of us staying behind to watch on the telescope. We needed someone to drop us off at the foothills and then be able to pick us up about twelve hours later. I decided to ask my daughter, Ashley, if she would provide the transportation. She said in order to be able to do it she would have to spend the night so she could be up by 4:00 a.m., our planned time of departure.

Today is Friday, Mike and I went to the airport to pick up Walter's son, Lars, in the late afternoon. His arrival was right on time. He came off the plane and saw Mike and me. He was full of excitement. Even though he is thirty-four years of age, he had the excitement of a little kid going to find a buried treasure. Lars thought it was as real as we knew it was. Mike and I showed up at Walter's house with Lars at about 6:00 p.m. We didn't stay too long Friday evening because Lars needed to spend some time with his father. We told Lars that we will be by in the morning sometime and that we had a lot of things to go over with him.

Friday night flew by quickly. Mike and I drove over to Walter's with all our information and photographs of our discoveries. Lars began to get more and more excited. Now we began to go over all the obstacles and dangers that we will be up against. Number one is safety; safety comes first. We told Lars that more than likely you're going to get jumping cactus stuck in your arms and legs. We told him it hurts and gets kind of bloody, but we knew how to deal with the jumpers and how to get them out quickly. My brother and I have experienced this many times and lived to tell about it. Then we told him about loose boulders and not to grab ahold of a boulder to lift your weight if it doesn't look too secure and to pay close attention to every step you take. Then we told him to keep your eyes open for any gunmen, rattlesnakes, scorpions and all other sorts of things in nature. The gunmen were one thing that we really had to keep our eyes and ears open for because of our previous experiences with them. That's one thing we will never forget. They are probably number one on our list of dangers.

Mike and I came up with a new plan to get up to the upper level of the gorge where we need to go. We are thinking it would be a short cut to save us time. We are hoping it will save us a couple of hours. We sat down and started to go over the new plan with Walter and his son. We told Walter we are going to need about two-hundred feet of rope strong enough to support our weight. Then since Lars was in excellent shape we wanted him to climb his way to that upper level. Then secure the rope around a cactus or boulder or whatever he could find, then throw the rope down to us so we could climb straight up the cliff instead of going all the way around like Mike and Walter did on the previous trip. We also told Walter we wanted a GPS locator so when we reach our discovery area we could write down the coordinates of where the discoveries are. The coordinates of our discoveries would actually be like a digital treasure map. So we went to Walmart and got the GPS locator and then stopped at a hardware store where we purchased two-hundred feet of very strong rope. We believe we have everything we would need including plenty of water and a few tools we might need.

Well we believe that we are all set and ready to go for the following morning. The date will be April 13, 2006.

CHAPTER 8

A HIGHER LEVEL OF FEAR

It was just a little over a week ago that we came close to death and now we are on our way again into the mountains. Unless they knew what was really there, nobody in their right mind would ever go back into the mountains so quickly just after coming so close to death during our previous trip.

It's Saturday night; my daughter, Ashley, just showed up to spend the night. Everyone is a little nervous and they tried not to show it. We know this must be done. The evidence is accumulating more and more after each and every trip. Who knows what we will discover on this trip? We set the alarm for 4:30 a.m. and went to bed to try to rest. Sleep did not come easy.

Once again the alarm is buzzing and now the phone is ringing. We had our coffee and began to pack our backpacks with plenty of water; doubling the amount of water so we don't have that problem again. You can live without food for a long time, but not water in that unforgiving wilderness. Walter called and said he was on his way and would be at Mike's house in five minutes. The truck pulled up and we quickly threw everything in the bed of the truck. Ashley got in the driver's seat and we were on our way. She dropped us off at the foothills and the four of us, Walter, Lars, Mike and I, were on our way into the mountains. We already know and expect to have blood all over our arms and legs. It happens every single time. Except now it will even be worse, because we're going all the way up to the upper level where the jumping cactus are so thick that it's almost impossible for them not to touch you. It almost seems like a video game and the object of the game is to make it in and out without being touched by the jumpers.

Lars couldn't believe it; it was his first trip ever going into the Superstition Mountains. Even though he was well aware of the dangers, he still loved it and was all excited about this once-in-a-lifetime adventure. As we are walking our way through the foothills heading for the south side of Tortoise Mountain, we begin to see the view of the cliff that we are about to make an attempt to climb up; using our strong rope. We all know that we've got to be a little crazy to attempt something like this. We don't even know what way or how we're going to get back down. We're definitely not planning on going down the same way we're going up. Without any experience at all in mountain climbing, it is far too dangerous going down feet first. First of all, we need to make it up there safely without someone getting killed. We know that the potential for someone getting seriously hurt or having a fatal accident is very real, but for our purposes we had to put it out of our minds and move forward.

We've made it out of the foothills and now entering the gorge south of Tortoise Mountain. It wouldn't be too long before we take a sharp left to start heading up this very steep and rough terrain. The cliffs that we will be climbing are at the top of this steep embankment. The closer we get the scarier it looks. The cliffs look a lot higher now then when you see them from a distance away. We begin thinking that we might not be able to do this after all, but we're still heading for the cliffs anyway. We want to see what they look like standing right in front of them before we make any decisions. I think that we're all shaking in our boots, but nobody would ever admit it. We finally made it up to the cliffs. We were all looking up at the cliffs saying how in the hell are we going to make it up there?

As we were examining the cliff, there was this area that had a crack that ran diagonally up the side of the cliff. If anyone wants to make an attempt and try to make it to the top, using the crack for a space for the feet, it was going to be Lars. Someone to help us get over the rockiest part of the cliffs, and where we are going there are a lot of obstacles. The first one will probably be the biggest obstacle of them all. That's to make it to the top of the cliff.

"I think, I can do it," Lars stated emphatically. "I would like to give it a try." We were all very nervous, especially his father. One wrong step and he could come crashing down to his death. Not only would he have broken bones, probably serious head injuries, but he also would tumble all the way down the very steep embankment that we had all just climbed up covering his body with jumping cactus from head to toe. So as Lars started climbing his way up very slowly, we all looked at each other shaking our heads saying, we can't believe that we are even doing this. Lars is also carrying his backpack that has the two-hundred feet of rope in it, plus the weight of the water and whatever tools he has in there.

We estimate his backpack weighs about 50 pounds. He's halfway up the cliff now and there's no turning back because coming down is a lot more difficult than going up. We can't believe what we are seeing; he's three quarters of the way up now and one slip and everything would be over. His dad has the cell phone in his hand ready to call 911 at any moment. Lars has about another twenty feet to go and then he will be safe. As the three of us are looking up at Lars with our eyes bugging out of our heads; our blood pressure was rising quickly with stress and worry. It was probably the most intense feeling for all of us in our lifetimes. Lars had just a few more feet to go. Then we watched as he pulled himself safely to the top of the cliff. What a relief it was for all four of us. Lars was probably more petrified than we were, even though we were far from being out of the woods.

One at a time the three of us have to climb up before this nightmare will come to an end. We are already nervous wrecks just from watching Lars and now it is our turn. The plan is, now that Lars has made it to the upper level, to secure the rope around a giant Saguaro cactus. "It is a ways back and I don't know if the rope is going to be long enough," Lars yelled back at us as he was walking to tie the rope around the cactus. He brushed up against a jumping cactus. The three of us heard him yelling something about he had jumping cactus stuck inside his arm. It was sounding very serious. We could hear the panic in his voice.

Walter began climbing up the cliff side. Not the same way that Lars had gone up, but a much harder climb. Mike and I looked at each other and said this is not looking good at all. This could turn into a disaster very easily now. Walter got about a third of the way up and then he couldn't go any farther and there was no way he could come back down. He was stuck on the side of this cliff holding on for dear life. Lars yelled down to us and said his arm was getting numb because the jumpers were working their way into his muscle and paralyzing it. Walter was panicking and yelling up to Lars to please hurry and secure the rope and throw it down to him as fast as possible. Mike and I both started yelling up to Lars and telling him to stop panicking and to ignore those jumpers and get a grip on yourself and focus on tying that rope around something and get it down to your dad as quick as you can. "So, move quickly Lars, your dad needs your help now!" We both were yelling. Lars finally began to listen and began to move real quickly even though he couldn't use his arm very well.

He found a cactus a ways back and quickly tied the rope around the base of it. Then he quickly went as close to the edge of the cliff and threw the rope over the cliff down to his father. The rope could not reach him. The cactus was too far back. Walter started to panic now. We were running out of time. Walter's legs started shaking. Walter again said in a panicky voice, "Please, Lars, hurry, I don't know how much longer I can hold on." Now Lars was panicking over maybe losing the father he loved. He quickly went as fast as possible to untie the rope tied around the cactus. He quickly went down closer to the edge and wrapped the rope around a boulder. It wasn't that big, but at least it was around something and he quickly threw the rope over the cliff. Luckily it landed very close to Walter where he was able to reach it.

Walter started pulling himself up the cliff sticking his foot in any hole he could find to help support his weight. He was slowly working his way up the cliff. As Mike and I were wiping the sweat off of our brows with great relief, Walter finally made it up where he then assisted his son to get the jumping cactus out of his arm. Mike and I waited down below as Walter was helping his son remove the dreaded cactus. As Mike and I were waiting down below we saw a humming bird. It was a light green color and it seemed like it was checking us out. It was the strangest thing; we had never seen a tiny humming bird come so close with such curiosity. Then the humming bird just flew off very quickly, as they often do. Walter removed all the fishhook type thorns from Lars' arm. Lars was so relieved.

Now it was time for one of the big guys to make it up the cliff. It was my turn. I weigh in at about 275 lbs. I am going to have to tie the rope around my chest and under my arms. Now Walter and Lars are going to have to pull me up the cliff. Lars threw the rope over the cliff and down to where Mike and I were standing. I grabbed a hold of the rope and then wrapped it around myself and tied about five knots in it to make sure it didn't come untied. Walter and Lars began to start pulling me up the cliff as I was looking for places to grab on to with my hands and places for my feet to help lift my weight. There was this one spot on the cliff that kind of like popped out towards me and they had to pull all my weight up and over that one spot. It took about ten to fifteen tries and then I finally got over it. Then they were able to pull me quickly up the rest of the way where it wasn't so vertical a climb.

Now it was Mike's turn. We threw the rope down to him. He tied it the same way I did around himself. This time there will be the three of us pulling Mike up the cliff. We counted to three and then began to pull Mike up the cliff. Then all of a sudden the humming bird reappeared. The bird was down on the cliff with Mike. Mike later said it was bouncing off his back as if to try to help him get up the cliff. Mike was coming up the cliff easily with the three of us on the other end of the rope. He finally made it up and all four of us were now at the upper level of the gorge. It was still very steep and we still had a ways to go to get to where we needed to be. The jumping cactus was in clusters everywhere. The terrain was very dangerous and rough. It took us over two hours for the four of us to make it up over the cliff.

The whole reason we wanted to go up and over the cliff was to save us about two hours of time. So we actually lost time instead of saving it. I guess we will never take that short cut again. But we would have never known unless we tried.

Off in a distance we could see the hole up on the side of the cliff where the carved, Arching Lady figure was on one side of the crevice and the carved priest on the other side where the hole is in between the two of them. Only one is visible at a time depending on what angle you are looking at it from and time of day. The main reason for this trip is to see if we could see anything up inside the hole. We brought the binoculars with us. We were hoping we could get close enough with the binoculars to see what was inside that hole. We needed to get there early enough so the sunlight would shine inside the hole.

The four of us needed to take a good break and replenish our bodies with plenty of water. We already knew that there wouldn't be enough time to try to make it over to the discovery of the Heart, where we believe the Peralta Treasure is located. We had no idea how long it would take us to find a way back down the mountain. It was already 11:30 a.m. and we still had quite a ways to go to get close to the hole. We knew we had to start looking for a way down the mountain by 1:00 p.m. We had an hour and a half to accomplish whatever we needed to do; and that was to see if we could see anything inside of that hole.

We continued our way up the steep dangerous embankment, working our way closer to the hole. To look inside it with the binoculars you can't be too close because the hole is on the side of a cliff. So we have to stay back far enough to look inside it. The sun is straight up above us now as it becomes noon time. There is shade inside the hole. We were hoping we would get there early enough so the sunlight was shining inside the hole. That was part of the reason why we wanted to take a shortcut to save a couple of hours. We finally made it up as far as we needed to be to see inside. We pulled out the binoculars and started looking at the hole. We couldn't see much of anything except a grayish background. The shade inside the hole made it to hard to see anything. That's if we can even find a way to get up there. By the looks of it we might need a thirty foot extension ladder. How good would that look if someone saw a few guys carrying a thirty foot extension ladder through the desert and up the mountains? The crazy thing about it is if we have to; we will. We're going to do whatever it takes to get the job done and hope we don't get killed in the process.

We have about forty minutes before we need to start looking for a way to get back down the mountain. So we work our way over to this mining area that we saw in our photographs from our previous trip. At least it looked like someone had done some mining. Maybe it was work from the Peraltas. Maybe they were just checking to see if there was any gold ore in that side of Tortoise Mountain. We walked over next to it and started checking it out. Someone definitely did some work here at one time, how long ago we don't know. We saw a large chunk of white ore stuck between a crack about fourteen feet up. Lars decided he would like to climb up to it and check it out. We still had a little time left. So Mike and I told Lars to go for it. Lars quickly climbed up to it and touched it. It was wedged in there pretty good, but while he was up there he said, "You know something there is something close by, I can feel it." Well, the Arching Lady and the priest are beside the hole that we were trying to look inside of was only forty-to fifty feet away, just around the corner.

We're so close, yet so far away because it was time for us to start descending back down the mountain. We have about six hours to get down the mountain before the sun goes down. It will be very slow going across the upper level of the gorge through the steep and rough terrain before we even start looking for a way down. We only need to go about four-or five hundred feet before we start looking for a way down. As bad as it is, that four-or five hundred feet to us will feel like we walked a few miles. All four of us are now badly beat up and totally worn out. We all have blood on our arms from scrapes, bushes with thorns and jumping cactus. The vultures are circling around us as they do when they smell the scent of blood.

We have now reached the area where we can start looking for a way down. There are a few very steep and rocky embankments that we could go down, but not all of them will bring us down and out of the mountain. Some of them will have cliffs about three quarters of the way down that we can't see from up here. So, what we decided to do was to send Lars down first to see if there was a way out; since Lars was in the best shape. Lars needed to use his own judgment because of the two big guys. Just because he might be able to get down a specific cliff, doesn't mean the two big guys can. So Lars went on down the embankment that looked most promising. He went about a third of the way down. Lars yelled up to us and said, "I think we can make it down through here." So the three of us began to try to navigate down the steep, rocky, brushy slope. Lars waited up for us to catch up with him. After we caught up with him, he went down another section of the very steep slope to see if it still looked promising to make it down that way. Lars yelled up to us again and this time he said it doesn't look good and he doesn't think we should attempt it.

He needed to come back up to us and try it from another angle from the same slope that we were on. He hoped we all didn't have to go all the way back to the top and start over, especially because of how tired and worn out we all are. Not to mention that the sun goes down in four and-a-half hours from now. When we start going down the wrong way that's when it starts to turn into a race against time. We have no time to waste.

Lars immediately went down the other side of the steep slope. He descended about one hundred feet to take a look. Again he yelled up to us just what we were hoping to hear. He said we shouldn't have any problems, but just making it down before the sun goes down is just one of our obstacles; we still have several others.

First of all, Walter came close to his death as he held on for dear life on that cliff. Second, the rock that the rope was tied on to for pulling up the two big guys could have given way. Third, just simply tripping on one of the many miniature cliffs and hitting our heads. Fourth, getting dehydrated. Fifth, Michael's health problems with his diabetes and high blood pressure could slow us down quite a bit.

Mike's having serious problems now descending he mountain with his heavy breathing. We make frequent stops for him to rest, not to mention his seriously damaged right knee that he has scheduled for an operation about 45 days from now. The pain in his knee is so bad that it constantly drives up his blood pressure. Sixth, rattlesnakes. There are so many rattlers and places for them to hide. At any time one could bite one of us on the leg. Seventh, Mountain Lions live in these mountains as mentioned before. For the last few days it's been on the news that mountain lions have been seen in people's backyards somewhere around the Superstition Mountains. When the drought kicks in, they are looking for water where ever they can find it. Those are just a few of the ways a person can and has died in these mountains. I forgot one, the gunmen. We always have a feeling that we are being watched by those men carrying guns. Mike and I know we're being watched. Walter is not sure about it. I just have to assume we are. Never rule it out. After all, we already have the proof in our photos.

As we descend the dangerous slope, we begin to see that we are going to make it down inside the center of the gorge where the wash is. Just knowing that we are going to make it that far is a relief.

The time is now 3:30 p.m. We have two and-a-half hours to get out of the mountains. That's about how long we figure it will take us. So there is no extra time for anything. The whole two and-a-half hours will be used up. Let's hope that nothing happens to any of us. Mike's breathing is getting very heavy now. Every fifty-to a hundred feet he needs for us to take a break. Five minute breaks are all we can afford, if that much, as sunset is quickly approaching. As hard as it is for Mike to breath he needs to fight it and just keep pushing himself. We all look like hell right now as all our energy has been totally drained from our bodies and blood all over our arms. If anyone was to see us right now they would probably think that we just played a role in that movie, *Night of the Living Dead.*

After another two hundred feet, we will be in the center of the gorge. Then we will be home free. As we get closer to the center of the gorge we can now see the giant "V". We will feel a sense of relief because we are familiar with the rest of the way out. This doesn't mean that we are out of the woods yet, because it's still very rough terrain until we reach the foothills. After a couple of short breaks we finally made it to the giant "V". We knew our way out from that point. It would be about an hour and-a-half before we reach the foothills. We were slowly working our way through the center of the gorge climbing over boulders and pushing our way through the thick brush and taking frequent breaks so Mike could catch his labored breath.

We are just reaching the foothills now. It's very close to sunset. The time is now 5:15 p.m. We will be calling for our pickup in Walter's truck in about thirty minutes. What a relief it is for all of us after a twelve-hour trip into those treacherous mountains. It's a quarter until 6:00 p.m. so we called Ashley, who was over at Walter's house, to come pick us up. We are watching the sun go down with just enough light to finish our way out of the foothills. Ashley pulled up with the truck on time. "Oh, my God you guys, you look half dead with all that blood on you" she said as soon as we climbed in the truck. None of us could even reply. We were so badly beat up from the twelve-hour trip. We all needed to get home and wash the blood off and drink some ice water and get some sleep.

Once I laid down on the couch I couldn't get back up. Every time I tried to stand up I had severe leg cramps all through my legs and then I would quickly have to lay back down. The same thing was going on with Lars, Mike and Walter. The next morning we were all very sore, but able to get up and start taking care of business. We did our regular routine and brought the film down for one-hour development. We were not expecting to find anymore evidence among the photos from this trip unless they reveal something inside that hole. We kind of doubted the photographs would show anything because the sun had passed over too far from it, leaving a shadow inside the hole. From our previous experience of other photos we had taken, shady spots would usually look black.

We went back to pick them up and straight to the computer to download the CD on Mike's computer. The computer was giving us trouble like always. With a little swift kick on the side of the computer it began to start downloading. Not bad for a computer that was being discarded. We began to start looking at the photographs. We brought up the photograph of the hole and tried to zoom inside with the photo enhancement and just as we thought it was too dark inside the hole. We looked at each other and said its okay, it doesn't matter. There is one good thing we got out of the trip and that was the experience. We now know the way down from the upper level. We don't have to search for a way down on our next trip. Therefore, it will allow us to have a little more time to try and make it to the discovery of the "Heart" inside the box canyon. We believe that all the evidence we need lies inside the box canyon. On the Peralta Stone Tablets, it shows a bull's eye in the center of the "Heart." If we are right, which we believe we are 100%, because of all our evidence that just keeps piling up, then one of the largest treasures in the world and the richest gold mines should be in the center of the heart inside the box canyon. We will never know the truth until we actually get inside the box canyon and get the close-up photos we need. Mike and I feel that even if we make it inside the boxed canyon, it's very clear to us, if we disturb it we will never make it out of the mountains alive. Then we will become the next victims of the curse and we are not about to let that happen.

This is why we believe that we have been chosen to end the curse and free all the lost souls that roam the Superstition Mountains, who died in vane over the same treasure that we are about to reveal to the world. We just hope and pray that we're right and we're doing just what the spirits want us to do. Time will tell as we continue our mission into the Superstition Mountains.

Lars keeps talking about how he will never forget the adventure he went on with his dad and two uncles. He said, "If I had the chance I would like to go up again with you." Mike and I said we'll see what happens. We will be planning our next trip into the Superstitions very soon. Probably sooner than you think.

Lars was flying back to New Hampshire in the morning and he

told us to let him know when our next trip would be. That he would possibly fly back out. Mike and I thought that would be great because he sure comes in handy when we get into some tough situations. Lars left for New Hampshire the following morning.

Mike and I knew we needed to start planning our next trip into the mountains. Somehow or some way we need to make it all the way to the heart inside the box canyon. That was our main focus. Mike and I talked about maybe spending the night once we reach the upper level of the gorge. But, because of the possibility of us being watched by gunmen and Mike's' health and other dangers, we decided that it might not be a good idea after all. We need to avoid certain situations or anything that could make us become the next victims of the curse. There are people in the Apache Junction area that would probably kill for the photographs of evidence we now hold secretly. Mike and I already know what's there in the center of the heart. We don't even need the close up; we already know. We just need the closeup photos to convince the public of our discovery. That's the only way that we know of that might possibly end the curse of the Lost Dutchman's Mine.

It's been a few days since our last trip into the mountains. We are just now fully recovering except for a few aches and pains. Now, we're already planning our next trip to try to make it all the way to the boxed canyon to get the photographs we need of the heart and close-ups of the very center of it. We're hoping that the center of the heart has some kind of a man-made wall and it's supposed to be a reddish rock that someone would have to destroy to break through it. So Mike and I are pretty anxious to get the job done and have all the evidence we need to prove our discovery is the real McCoy, the treasure that everyone has been searching for over a hundred some-odd years.

Mike and I made a plan for this following Monday coming up. Lars told us to let him know when the next trip would happen. We don't think he is expecting it so soon. Therefore, he might not be able to go due to his wife and kids needing him at home. We are going to call him anyway. We hope he says he can go with us; that would be great. With or without him, Mike and I will get the job done somehow. When we called Lars and told him what was up he couldn't believe that we were heading back up so soon, but he was all excited and said he had to talk to his wife first and that he would call us back within the hour. He called us back with excitement in his voice saying, "I can go, but my wife isn't too happy about it." He said he would be back on a plane this weekend. Lars called us back the next day and said that his church was going to let him borrow a video camera. He said it was a real nice one. Mike and I thought that would be great to video the whole trip into the mountains.

Now that Mike and I know we're going to be bringing a video camera we need to set some kind of a plan for a documentary. That's going to take some thinking, because neither of us have any experience doing a documentary. We will have to just do the best we can. I guess I'm going to do the narrating for the documentary. I'm not expecting to do a professional job; all I can do is give it my best shot. With our sense of humor it might turn out to be more of a comedy than a documentary.

Mike and I had to come up with a new plan on how we're going to make it up to the upper level of the gorge. We were definitely not going back up that cliff again. We are so lucky to be alive after that last episode on the cliff, so we'll just stay away from that. We do have another place on our mind, not too much farther over from the cliff.

We have been pretty close to this one area before. It's up at the top of this very steep rugged embankment. There's a small cliff up at the top about twenty feet high. It does look climbable, even for the two big guys. We're not sure what it looks like up above the twenty foot cliff. That won't be a problem because we will let Lars go first to see what it looks like up above the small cliff. Lars will know if it will bring us the rest of the way up. We hope we don't have to use the rope. We are still black and blue under our arms from the last trip.

Lars will arrive on Saturday from New Hampshire and Monday morning we will be on our way once again into those devastating mountains. Of course, we get a little nervous and sick to our stomachs just thinking about it. After all, we come close to death just about every time we go into the mountains. We're from New England and we're not used to this type of stuff, mountain climbing and such. At least we have a little experience under our belts from our previous trips.

Today, Thursday, Mike and I will be picking Lars up at the airport again this coming Saturday afternoon. We decided that we needed to relax for a couple of days to get rid of the aches and pains. Those couple of days went by really quickly. It's Saturday and we're off to the airport again to pick up Lars. His flight arrived on time. We went straight to his Father's house. Walter was not able to go into the mountains with us on Monday because he would be gone on business. It will only be the three of us. Lars showed us the video camera. It was a very nice one. We started playing around with it so we could learn how to use it. We learned that it had a zoom on it. Mike and I looked at each other and thought the same thing. When we get to the upper level in the gorge over by the priest and the Arching Lady carved in stone, we will be able to zoom inside the hole. We hope we can see something inside; especially because it is the same place that the priest is pointing the cross.

I don't know about Mike but I'm a little sick to my stomach just thinking about where we are going tomorrow morning. We know we have to get this done whether we like it or not. We rounded up a few photographs to lay out on the kitchen table for in the morning. We had photos of the Peralta Stone Tablets and also one of the Arching Lady on the table. To start off our documentary, we want to aim the video at the photos, then get in the truck and start heading for the mountain, video taping Tortoise Mountain as we get closer and closer towards it until we get dropped off. Then continue video taping everything from the foothills all the way to the upper level of the gorge.

CHAPTER 9

WHERE THE TURTLE BURIED ITS EGGS

It was Sunday evening and the alarms were set for 4:30 a.m. Monday morning. Since Walter was gone on business we had to depend on his wife, Debra, to drive us to the foothills to drop us off and then pick us back up about twelve hours later. The night went by in a flash. It was time. The alarms started buzzing and phones started ringing. It was the same routine. We had our coffee and then grabbed our backpacks and headed over to Walter's house where we would begin to start filming. Lars was up and raring to go. We made sure the photos were lined up right on the kitchen table. We then handed the video camera over to Debra so she could get the three of us on film. Then I took the video camera from her and began to start filming the photographs on the kitchen table. Then I shut off the video camera and we all got in the truck and started heading for Tortoise Mountain. I quickly turned the video camera back on as we drove towards the mountain getting closer and closer. We then turned on the radio so we could have some music recording on the video tape as well. We thought that would give the documentary a good effect. The song that came on the radio was the perfect song for the beginning of the documentary. We didn't know the name of the song at the time; we now know the name is, *DON'T DREAM IT'S OVER*, by Crowded House. We just knew the song sounded great. The words of the song were saying "Hey, now, hey, now," and then the words were talking about a wall that needed to be torn down that we were up against, or something to that effect. We were to learn more about the song later. The song seemed like it was meant to be.

We pulled up to the foothills to where Debra would drop us off. We got out of the truck and began our seventh journey into the Superstition Mountains; filming the jumping cactus that were all around us. It was still a little dark out because the sun hadn't come up over the mountains yet, but it was light enough to see where we were going. Before too long we were getting close to the mouth of the gorge. We took a good ten minute break and then continued on. It was important to get as far as we could go while it was nice and cool out and before the sun came over the mountain. We were making very good time so far. But we knew once we get into the steep and rough terrain we will have to slow down as it gets very dangerous. As we entered the gorge we looked over to the left at the cliff we climbed on during our previous trip and still couldn't believe we had climbed up over that and are still here to talk about it. But in reality it doesn't matter which way we go to get to the upper level of the gorge; it's all very, very dangerous. It's been about two hours now and we're about to bear to the left and start heading up a very steep and very dangerous slope. It's the same slope that Mike and I went up on our very first trip into the mountains. We just never went up over the twenty foot cliff up at the top that we are going to attempt today.

No matter how hard we try to stay away from the jumpers they always find a way to get on us. Of course, we all have a little blood on us already, it's perfectly normal to us now and we're used to it and we know what we're going to look like by the end of the day, if we make it out of here alive. We know that we're pushing our luck every trip we make into the mountains. The video tape is rolling as we ascent the steep and dangerous slope. Jumpers are everywhere all around us. At this point and time they're our number one obstacle. We can see the twenty foot cliff about seventy-five feet up at the top of the embankment that we were on. That will be our next major obstacle that we are about to encounter. That will be our next break before we make an attempt to go up and over it.

We now have made it up to the cliff where we are now standing in front of it. We will take our fifteen minute break before we make the attempt to go up and over it. We all drank a bottle of water each to be sure we are staying hydrated. Now it's time as Lars will be the first to go up and over it to see what it looks like and to see whether or not we can continue on from up above. Once us two big guys get up top of the twenty foot cliff there's no turning back, because we can't go back down feet first.

That's why it's so important that Lars makes the right decision whether or not we can continue on once we're up top of the cliff. We don't want to get trapped up there with no place to go because, of course, we will have no choice but to call search and rescue. Lars began to climb up the twenty foot cliff. He started working his way diagonally across the four inch crack. There was a four inch lip sticking out that he was able to walk on going in a diagonal direction across the ledge with the possibility of a 400 foot roll down the canyon. This is where a cactus would be a pleasure if it stopped you from falling any further. He made it across with no problem where he then boosted himself up and over a rock that was at the right side of the cliff. He was now at the top of the cliff. He started looking at what was ahead of us and what he could see was another very rocky rough slope that looked to him like it was climbable even for us. Lars said it looks like it will bring us all the way to the upper level. The two of us had to go with his judgment and began to climb in the same diagonal direction that Lars climbed. We both followed each other at the same time. Mike and I realized that this was no comparison to the previous trip we made when we were hanging with ropes on the great big cliff. We were a little slower than Lars, but were getting there. We finally made it all the way to the right hand side where we then boosted our weight up and over that rock and made it safely up above the twenty foot cliff.

We now took another fifteen minute break and I just started filming all around us to show what it looked like up top of the cliff. Then we passed the camera back and forth to get each one of us on film. Then we each drank a bottle of water and then continued on up the slope that was so treacherous. Some parts of that slope was like walking on marbles. Our feet were always sliding out from underneath both of us because of the millions of tiny rocks. So far everything was looking good that we could see ahead of us, as far as making it to the upper level. It is now 10:00 a.m. and we had been hiking for four hours by then. We had a total of three more hours to get the job done before we have to start descending back down the mountain. Thank God, we knew the way down from our previous trip. Experience makes a real difference. Just knowing the way down helps us to be able to concentrate more on the task at hand instead of worrying how we're going to get back down. We finally made it to the top of the slope and there's this one area that we took a break at on our last trip. It actually looks like it could be used for a landing pad for a helicopter, even though the authorities would never allow that to happen.

If a helicopter could be used it sure could save a lot of mountain climbing and we would have all the time in the world to get the job done, but that's okay because we're just dreaming. It will never happen. The wreckage of two planes had been discovered and they are still in the mountains today.

We are all very exhausted now and Michael's breathing is getting very heavy and his knee is in extreme pain. He continuously tries to ignore it and our arms and legs have blood all over them, but not as bad as previous trips. It's like a video game the more you play it the better you get with higher scores. From a distance, we can now see the hole where the priest and the Arching Lady are.

I turned the video camera on and began to start filming all around us again and down at the city of Apache Junction. We were way up high looking down over the city. Then I tried to zoom inside the hole and I couldn't believe it, I brought the hole right up to the camcorder and could actually zoom in close enough to maybe see what was inside the hole. So I did that about four different times zooming right inside the hole. If I got any closer I might not have been able to see what was deeper inside the hole, because of it being on the side of the cliff at an angle. I was glad to have gotten the shots that I did get from that distance. Mike and I were so beat up from all that climbing that we couldn't make it down and then up inside the box canyon where our discovery of the heart is.

Lars was capable of reaching the box canyon and if he was going to make it down inside the canyon he had to start heading in that direction now. We had no time to waste. So Lars headed off in the direction of the boxed canyon by himself. Mike and I also went in that direction until we could find a place that wasn't too far away from him and be able to video tape him down inside the box canyon. He had an hour and-a-half to get the job done to get the photographs that we needed to prove to ourselves that we had been right all along about what we believed was in the center of the heart; one of the richest and largest treasures in the world; the Peralta treasure and possibly where the Lost Dutchman got his rich ore from.

Lars was working his way slowly down inside the boxed canyon. He was almost at the mouth of the box canyon where it was very steep and dangerous. He had his digital camera with him to take still photos. We told him as soon as he got inside the canyon to start taking photographs of everything and all around at every angle possible so if there were gunmen around watching us, they wouldn't see us focusing in on one single location and lead them to the riches.

So we are trying to be careful on how we handle this whole situation. A little psychology comes in very handy when you're dealing with the good guys and the bad guys. It didn't take long for the good guys to find the treasure. The problem is that the bad guys have been searching all their lives for what took us only weeks to discover. That's why Mike and I feel that we have been spiritually led and that the treasure was just given to us on a gold platter. What other reason could there be when we're not after the gold and treasure. We just want to free the spirits that died in vane searching for it. We want to end the curse of the Lost Dutchman Mine and expose it to the world. It is what the final outcome of this whole situation ends up being, which we don't know what that is yet. Only the spirits know where this is leading.

Lars was now down inside the box canyon, just at the mouth of it taking a break getting ready to go inside and begin taking the photographs. Mike and I know now that as long as we make it out of the mountains safely, this was going to be a success. We were very excited with Lars making it down in the boxed canyon. Mike worked his way up to the mine area that we had found on one of our previous trips. It looks as though whoever was mining it was probably looking for a vein of gold or silver. It was probably done in the mid 1800s. We can only imagine it was either the Peraltas or Jacob Waltz who did the work, but did not find anything unless there's something there and we just aren't seeing anything yet. Our main focus today is to take close-up photos of the center of the heart and get some kind of evidence telling us there's something in that hole where the priest and Arching Lady are.

Lars is now further up inside the boxed canyon. He's close enough to begin taking photographs. He started shooting the photos. Starting at one end of the boxed canyon and working his way around taking photos of everything. He took photographs of the heart from all different angles including the center of the heart, which on the Peralta Stone Tablets would be the bull's-eye, and that would be the storage compartment of one of the treasures or gold veins or maybe even both of them together. One way or another it would be the bonanza. The one that all the treasure hunters died searching for in the last 150 years. So Lars went from one end of the boxed canyon to the other taking all of the photographs we needed. Now, it was time for him to start heading back up to where Mike and I are waiting for him. The time is now 12:45 p.m. We need to start descending the mountain by 1:00 p.m. Lars has quite a ways to go to get back where Mike and I are. So, we will probably be a little late leaving the area. At least we know the way down this time. This will save us a lot of time.

If we leave by 1:30 p.m., we should still be okay.

It's been about 20 minutes since we last spoke to Lars. We can't see him because of this great big long natural wall that divides us from the boxed canyon. Mike and I began yelling down to Lars so we could find out where he was. We didn't get an answer. We started getting a little nervous. We waited a few more minutes and then we called out his name again and there was still no answer. Mike and I had panic written all over our faces. All we could hear was our voices echoing all throughout the gorge. If there was anyone else besides us, they would have certainly heard us for sure. We were drawing a lot of attention to ourselves as we were panicking for Lars' safety. Then just a moment or two later we heard Lars' voice echo throughout the gorge. We called out his name one more time just to be sure. He answered us back as he was climbing his way out of the boxed canyon.

Mike and I were worried sick. It was such a relief to hear his voice. As soon as he reached the point where Mike and I were we would take a short break and then start to descend the mountain. Lars made it back to where Mike and I were by the mining area. Just for the hell of it, I picked up Lars backpack just to see how heavy it was. It had to have weighed at least 60 pounds. I couldn't believe he went all the way to the boxed canyon and back with it. Lars said, "I hope I got the photographs you guys are going to need." He said that he took photos of every surrounding cliff inside the box canyon. Mike and I were confident that this trip was going to be a huge success. We were so excited and we hadn't even started back down the mountain yet. The time was 1:30 p.m. We had about four and-a-half hours to descend the mountain before the sun goes down. We started down the mountain. Thank God, this time we knew our way down. We headed down the same slope we went down on the last trip. It was very steep and dangerous, but at least we knew the way. It would bring us down to the lower level of the gorge where the giant "V" was. We were making better time than the last trip down the mountain, especially after that long break Mike and I had while we waited for Lars to come back from the boxed canyon. Our arms were covered with blood from the jumpers and the vultures could smell it as they flew circles around us up above. All of a sudden we heard a rattle and the three of us froze. There was a rattlesnake very close to us somewhere. We did not want to move until we knew it was safe. So, with our walking sticks, we were reaching out and touching the bushes to see if the snake would rattle and sure enough it did. Now we were able to walk in the opposite direction to go around the snake and continue on. We didn't have very much experience dealing with rattlesnakes. We've only encountered one other snake before this, when Mike and Walter ran into a giant Diamondback on one of the previous trips.

The time was now 4:15 p.m., we have almost made it as far as the giant "V." In two hours the sun will be going down over the horizon. We don't have much time for breaks, even though Mike is in a lot of pain with his knee and of course his breathing is heavy as always. As crazy and tough as it is in the Superstitions, it's still so very exciting no matter how much blood we had on us or how many vultures are flying in circles up above us waiting for their next meal.

We are finally at the giant "V." I pulled out the binoculars and took a good look around to be sure there wasn't any unexpected visitors, but I always feel like someone is watching us. I don't know if its just paranoia because of the gunmen we encountered before or what. We just can't rule out the possibility of gunmen hiding behind rocks with guns to our backs. To be honest, I don't think they would shoot us unless they saw us pulling out treasure from somewhere up here, or unless they knew that we knew where there was one. Then they might possibly put guns to our heads and tell us to take them to where the treasure is. Anything like this is possible, especially in the Superstition Mountains. Apache Junction is loaded with treasure hunters that would be dammed if a couple of New Englanders would come out here and rip it out from underneath them, especially when they have been searching all of their lives for this treasure. Just a four hour trip when we saw the yellow square.

We won't know for sure until we develop the film of the pictures that Lars took inside the box canyon. If that treasure is there in the center of the heart, these photos that we took will tell us everything. Today is the big day. The day we've been waiting for; to finally make it inside the box canyon. Our legs feel like rubber as we are working our way closer to the foothills. Every 50-to 100 feet we take a quick break so Mike can catch his breath; its 5:15 p.m. We have 45 minutes before the sun goes down. We entered the foothills and then we called Debra and told her to pick us up in 20 minutes. The three of us made it out of the foothills and were waiting at our pick-up location. We saw the truck pass by a couple of times down at the end of the road. Being Debra's first time giving us a ride, she must've gotten lost. So we started walking down the road where we could flag her down next time she passed by. As drained and beat up as we were from our devastating 12 hour trip into the mountains, this was the last thing we wanted was for our ride not to be there when we got out of the foothills. She finally saw us and we flagged her down. We were not mad but just happy that we made it in and out of the Superstitions safely without any injuries or heart attacks. As bad a shape as we were in, we still went straight to Walgreens to drop off the film. We decided to pick the film up the next morning instead of the one-hour development. We all went home to get cleaned up and get some rest and then the leg cramps started in. We were expecting the leg cramps, it happens every time. We would eventually get over the leg cramps after a good night's rest. The next morning we went to Walgreens and picked up our photos and CD while Lars was over at his father, Walter's, making us a copy of the documentary tape that we filmed. We couldn't wait to watch that on Mike's large TV and also see the photographs of inside the box canyon, with our main focus being the center of the heart. We've had all kinds of exciting things happening now and we were still alive to see it. We went to work trying to download the CD on Mike's computer and got it done with a little swift kick to the side of the computer. It began to download the CD. All of the photographs began popping up one at a time. There must have been at least 50 photographs and all of them were inside the boxed canyon. We had a lot of studying to do, at least for the next week. Each photograph needs to be examined very closely, because we know how the different shapes can fool a person especially photographs of the Superstition Mountains. Being close-ups inside the box canyon, there shouldn't be too much fooling going on. Whatever we see will most definitely be real without a doubt. Mike and I already know that the bonanza treasure from the Peralta's is in the center of the heart. We just want to know what the sealed entrance looks like. We are about to find out right now as we are looking through the photos. We can't see the whole heart because Lars is so close and standing right in front of it as he took the pictures. All we're seeing are the sections of the heart

This reddish door with ramp shape in front at the center of our discovery Heart represents the bull's-eye on the front of the insert heart.

and that is exactly what Mike and I wanted to see. The markings and the symbols are unbelievable, not just what's in the heart, but all over inside the boxed canyon. As we are quickly going over all of the photos we saw this one photo that caught our attention real quick. It was the center of the heart. Just what we've been waiting to see. Mike and I just looked at each another and said, "There it is, just what we suspected all along." It was a hasty square wall that was red in color. It almost looks like a door with a seam all the way around it. Mike and I remember what the directions said that were addressed to Jacob Waltz. The last words on those directions were, "Destroy the red rock." In the same photograph the yellow square is to the upper left with the black stripe mineral deposit running down over it. We can see the date 1847 just above the black stripes. There is also some kind of symbol that looks kind of like a bird, its black and has two wings. We've no idea what the bird symbol means yet, but we imagine we will find out sooner or later as we keep studying the photos and doing more research on the Peraltas. As I was looking at the yellow square just to the upper left of the red hasty wall, I saw a Spanish treasure symbol. One of the Spanish treasure symbols that I learned about up in the Goldfield Mountains that Paul told me about and showed pictures of. It was a symbol of the sun and the wildest thing about this treasure symbol of the sun was that it had an eyeball in the center of the symbol and it was staring straight at the red hasty wall with the cross on it. As we were looking through some of the other photographs of a different area in the boxed canyon, we came across this one photo and it looked like a 12-to 15 foot cross carved out of the cliff showing Jesus nailed to the cross and just to the left of the giant cross it looked like there was another man carved out of the cliff that was being crucified by someone holding a pitchfork. And then another very strange thing, just to the right of the giant cross was a girl poking her head up staring straight at us or actually was staring at Lars when he was taking the photographs. But a crazy thing about it was the girl didn't look like she was alive but maybe a spirit or something like that. There was definitely something going on involving the supernatural.

The bird symbol looks like a bird in flight. The symbol is also seen around our other many discoveries. There is an enormous amount of symbols in our photos, very large to very small. We believe this would take a large amount of people many years.

This Spanish treasure symbol of the sun with an eye in the center of it, staring at the bull's-eye (door) in the center of the discovery heart.

The image of a man we believe to be Jesus which appears to be attached a structure that looks like a cross. It's almost looks too real.

Picture of a women that appears to be spiritual, poking her head up below the Jesus figure on cross.

Mike and I are now realizing that this boxed canyon is not just a place where someone hid a treasure, but a very sacred place. A place where people gathered to worship Jesus and used this boxed canyon in a way like a church and the treasure in the center of the heart is more than likely offerings to the church and Jesus Christ. The same way they pass the basket around in church for the people to give offerings to the church. We don't know for sure, but that's the picture that Mike and I are getting from looking at the photos. All these close up photographs are just revealing so much to us now and giving us more of an understanding what actually was going on inside this boxed canyon. I began looking at the photo that had the center of the heart at the red hasty wall with a square shape to it, when all of a sudden I spotted something. I could make out the shape of a turtle 15- to 20 feet wide with the head and the shell with his little pointed tail. The head has an eye and his little mouth carved right into it.

The first thing that came to my mind when I saw this was what I read in a book when I lived in the Goldfield Mountains. It said, "Where the turtle buries its eggs you will find the treasure." Well, it looks like we found out where the turtle buried its eggs. The only problem is the eggs are going to have to stay buried behind that red hasty wall because my brother and I are definitely not going to disturb this, because its not ours to disturb. It would be like reaching our hand in the basket at church and stealing the offerings. And besides, Mike and I know that if we even attempted to remove any of this treasure we would never make it out of the mountain alive. Maybe there's other treasures in the mountain like gold bars and nuggets that a person could get away with, but not this one. Because there's way too many spiritual powers and dealing with the supernatural for anyone to think they could just walk out of the mountain with this treasure. That's the very reason why nobody has ever lived that planned and tried to remove this treasure. There's a reason why Mike and I were led to this treasure; we know that it wasn't meant for us to just take the treasure and run. We believe that there is a spiritual reason behind this whole deal and someday soon we will find out what that reason is. We don't need any more evidence to prove to ourselves the treasure really exists behind the red hasty wall that's on the center of the heart. All the markings are there. Including the priest and mother Mary, who we believe is the Arched Lady holding baby Jesus and the Spanish treasure symbol with the eye in the center of it staring at the red hasty wall in the center of the heart, which would be the bulls-eye on the Peralta Stone Tablets. Mike and I have realized that if we try to tell someone about our discovery they think that we are absolutely crazy, because of all of the people that claimed they have discovered The Lost Dutchman's Mine over the last 100 years. Mike and I say one thing that nobody else has ever claimed, that they have solved

This is a large turtle that is just above the door in the center of the discovery heart, where the turtle buried it's eggs. The golden eggs are about to be fried.

the mystery of the Peralta Stone Tablets. There's been people who claimed they knew where the heart was but had no evidence to back it up. That's because there are 1000s of heart shapes in the Superstition Mountain Wilderness. But there is only one true heart that portrays the Peralta Stone Tablets and to find this one and only true heart would be nothing short of a miracle. For a person to find the skull fragment that belonged to Adolph Ruth in such a large area of the mountain would also take a miracle. To find the priest carved out of stone that portrays the Priest Tablet and the Arching Lady holding baby Jesus would also be a miracle. How could so many miracles happen to Mike and me? Not to mention all of the coincidences that happened when we first stepped foot into the mountains and not believe we were spiritually led.

It was June 6, 2006. Today is my birthday, 06-06-06. I was at Mike's house when I decided to grab the folder that held all our photographs. I was looking through them and one photograph caught my eye immediately. It was a cave where Mike found the skull fragment on the ground outside the entrance of the cave. To the right of the cave, I began to see the image of a horse. I could see his eye and ears and the rest of his body, including his tail. The horse was staring across the gorge in the same direction as our treasure location. Then Mike got a photograph of the stone tablet that had the Horse of Santa Fe on it. We then placed the photographs next to each other to make a comparison. Sure enough, it looked like a match. Because of all of the other evidence we accumulated, we had to believe that it was the horse that was portrayed on "the Horse of Santa Fe tablet." We were able to locate all of the symbols that were on the tablet surrounding the horse, including the initials J.W., which we translated to be Jacob Waltz' initials. Was this just another coincidence?

On September 5th, our sister, Patty called us from Gloucester, Massachusetts. She told us that she was coming to Apache Junction on vacation to visit us and wanted us to take her up to the treasure location. Patty told us about a song we needed to hear. It was about the wall that we were up against. We were all excited about her letting us hear the song.

On September 26th, our sister, Patty arrived on vacation. Again, Patty mentioned that song and she couldn't wait to let us hear it. Mike

The Horse of Santa Fe Stone Tablet

Above the cave, where Jacob Waltz left his initials and Adolph Ruth's alleged Skull fragment was found, to the right in front of the cave stands the carved Horse of Santa Fe looking in the direction of what Miguel Peralta called one of the largest treasures in the world. The treasure is about 200 yards across.

and I started telling Patty about our documentary we filmed up in the Superstitions about our discovery. We told her we wanted her to watch it on TV.

About four days later, we made a plan to watch our documentary and listen to the song Patty wanted us to hear.

That evening we all went to Mike's house. We decided to watch the documentary first before hearing the song. Mike placed the tape, which was the only tape we had on hand, the one without sound, in the recorder when Patty experienced her first spiritual encounter. We began to watch the tape when we got about a third of the way through the tape, when the picture of us climbing the mountain suddenly started to scramble. Flashes of an old man with gray hair and a mustache kept appearing and disappearing. Then the picture turned black. Mike suddenly got up and tried to restart the tape in the VCR. All of a sudden it flashed back to us going up the mountain and then became scrambled again and these two large eyes filled the screen. During this episode, everybody was frantic and Patty was screaming, "Who is that old man?" Mike then grabbed another tape that we had, except this one had the sound to it. We told our sister Patty that this one has a song on it that was recorded off the radio in the truck when we began the documentary heading off to the mountain. We told her that it was the most perfect theme song for the documentary. Then Mike put the tape in and began to play it. As soon as the theme song came on Patty started screaming, "Oh, my God, that's the song I brought with me that I wanted you guys to hear. Was this another sign that we were spiritually led or was it just another coincidence? Then Mike said, "What are the chances for something like this to happen; for our nephew to wake his mother up in the middle of the night to hear this song and to bring it to Arizona with her, because of our discoveries and then for it to be the same song that was playing on the radio?" This would have to be added to the list of miracles.

How many miracles would it take for a person that was in our situation to be convinced that it's no longer just a coincidence and the only alternative would be that the supernatural was involved. Patty enjoyed her stay, but it was now time for her to return to her home.

On February 20th 2007, my brother Walter and I took a drive all around the edges of the mountain. When all of a sudden I heard this voice in my head telling me to climb to the top of Silly Mountain, which was approximately four miles away from our discovery of the treasure. So Walter and I hiked all the way to the top of Silly Mountain and we could actually see the exact location where the treasure was. Luckily, Walter brought his camera with him. Walter took out his camera and started zooming in on the treasure location from four miles away and then just started snapping pictures. Silly Mountain is a very small mountain that sits all by itself in the desert of Apache Junction. I said to myself why do the spirits want me to climb such a small mountain especially when it was four miles away from our treasure discoveries.

And then Walter and I descended Silly Mountain and went home like it was no big deal. The next day Walter went to Walgreens to have the film developed. It was just a few pictures of our discovery site from four miles away. We were not expecting anything much out of the photographs. Walter picked up the photographs from Walgreens along with a CD and went home and downloaded the CD on his computer and printed out some 8x10 photos. Walter handed me over a couple of the 8x10 photos and as soon as they were placed in my hand I immediately realized that another miracle had just happened. It was the image of a lion, with his front left leg wrapped around our discovery of the heart and treasure as though the lion was protecting the Church of the Holy Faith and its treasure that still exists there today. I had no idea about the lion and what the lion represented. I had a little research to do on this lion. Because of the whole situation and what is involved here, my first place to start looking would be the Bible. Paul was back in town going to Cobbs Restaurant for coffee at night. If there was anybody that knew about the lion and what it represented, it would be Paul. I knew I could count on Paul for this type of information, especially because of what's involved here. So that evening I went to Cobbs to see Paul.

Already aware of the discovery that my brother, Mike, and I had made, he said, "Well, Bill I guess we know the reason why you were brought to me up in the Goldfield Mountains" I said, "It's amazing how powerful the spirit world is." Paul replied, "It's far from over, they have a much bigger plan in the works." Then I asked Paul the

The lion has it's left leg wrapped around the discovery heart protecting what it believes to be a sacred treasure. Look carefully and you can still see the line of dots from 4 miles away.

On April 17, 2006 a shadow in the shape of a lion was on the front page of the local A.J. Newspaper. The shadow is leaping out of the discovery heart.

question, "Paul, what is the deal with the lion? I need information about the lion." Paul just laughed and walked out to his car to get his Bible. Paul came back in the restaurant and sat down, then opened up his Bible. He knew exactly where to go in the Bible. Within one minute he found the page. He began to read it to me. It said "Under the title of the scroll and the lamb I saw a scroll in the right hand on the one who sits on the throne. It was covered with writing on both sides and was sealed with seven seals. And I saw a mighty angel, who announced in a loud voice, who is worthy to break the seals and open the scroll but there was no one in heaven or on earth or in the world below who could open the scroll and look inside it. I cried bitterly because no one could be found who was worthy to open the scroll or look inside it. Then one of the elders said to me, "Don't cry, look, the lion from Judah's tribe, the great descendant of David has won the victory, and he can break the seven seals and open the psychological." As I was sitting at the table with Paul, he told me that he had been reading a book called *Eckvida*, the ancient science of prophesy and it also talked about the lion and what it represents. Paul began to read it to me. It said, "The lion is the ancient symbol of gold and often represented the sun gods, such as M.I.T.H.R.A.S., in Egypt of the olden days it was believed that the lion presided over the annual floods of the Nile River, because the floods coincided with the entry of the sun into the zodiacal sign of Leo during the dog days. The lion has been used for many symbols, for rivers and despots who believed themselves the king of the people, corresponding with the lion as the king of the beasts. The mountain is attached to symbolism, because it is equated with the inner leftness of the spirit." What Paul has just read to me from the Bible and the *Eckvida* book open up a much broader view of all of the possibilities of what could be going on here with my brother's and my discovery. Of course, people are going to have their own opinions and see different views including my brother. It is possible that Adolph Ruth got too close to the Peralta treasure, but was not worthy enough to open it up and lost his life because of it. Who knows how many people lost their lives over the Peralta treasure in the last 150 years because they stuck their nose in the wrong place, not realizing that this place is highly protected by the higher power and the supernatural, which would possibly be what treasure hunters believe is the curse. That this place is just protected from people that have their greed for gold and money. Why are my brother, Mike, and I still alive? That's a question that's always on my mind. It is because spirits in the mountains already know that Mike and I would not try to remove this treasure, but instead carry out the plan that they have in store for us: That would one day benefit the higher power. Only the higher power knows the real truth and what the final outcome of this story will be. I can say this, from when our first journey into the Superstition Mountains began, or up until now a year and-a-half later my life has changed dramatically. It has woke me up and made me much more aware of the good and evil. There's a lot of good in the world, but evil is on the warpath. From when I began writing this manuscript, it seems like I've been up against a wall. As though some evil force is trying to prevent this book from happening. It has been a nonstop fight all the way from day one until now and is only getting worse. If this book ever makes the bookstores, I would have to say it would be another miracle. If you only knew the battle that I'm up against, you would understand. What my brother, Mike and I are about to explain is just a portion of the wall we are up against.

CHAPTER 10

WILL THE TRUTH STAY HIDDEN

Mike wrote a brief outline to the East Valley Tribune, in Mesa, Arizona in a latest attempt to go public with our story. The reply was almost immediate. Within hours Mike was talking with one of the Tribune reporters. The reporter told Mike that it was very interesting and he wanted to climb the mountain to see exactly what we had found. Mike asked him if he would like to see some physical proof. He replied, "I don't need to see any evidence right now, but I would like to climb the mountain as soon as tomorrow morning. Mike told him he could not give him a time right away, that he'd have to talk to his brother, Bill, first. Mike began to tell him some of the evidence we had, for example, 20 plus photographs of evidence, self-made documentary, two local newspaper articles on the alleged Adolph Ruth skull fragment. Again he declined and did not desire any physical evidence. The next day Mike and I talked. We decided the trip would be on Monday, four days away. Mike called the reporter and asked him if Monday would be fine for him. He replied that Monday would be fine and he'd like to bring a photographer. Mike and I decided that would be okay. The reporter and the photographer showed up first thing Monday morning as planned. We greeted them properly, then started to discuss the trip that preceded us. Then Mike and I began telling them that our intentions were to expose the answers to the Peralta Stone Tablets. We asked them to come inside while we waited for our transport. We then showed them some pictures so they could see the type of dangerous terrain we had to deal with. Then our transportation arrived as planned, and we headed off into the Superstition Mountains. We arrived about 3/4 of a mile from the base of the mountain. We stood looking up a long and slightly vertical hike to the base of the mountains. It had steep mountain sides that make up what look like a gigantic horseshoe. They call it Monument Pass. It is very, very dangerous. Finally, we start our assent up the mountains. The reporter starts firing questions as we volunteered more information. The photographer started shooting pictures, first at us, then as we started pointing out the locations of our discoveries, as he photographed our several months of research and then ten life threatening explorations. At this time we could only wonder how they will print such a huge story. We had told the reporter earlier in order to print the whole story with definitive pictures, they would have to alert certain local state and federal governments. It would have to be a controlled release to avoid a stampede into the mountains. After showing them everything we had discovered everyone was in a hurry to get down, water was low and temperatures were high. Even though we did not take them all the way to the upper level of the gorge, the photographer had a telescopic lens and was able to get some pretty good photos of our discovery especially as we descended the mountain and then into the foothills when we then called for our transport for pick up. Our transport pick up was on time and within a short time we were at Mike's house. Everyone came inside to enjoy a cold glass of herbal sun tea. We sat down in Mike's living room. Mike already had a table all set up to display our indisputable evidence. What the reporter and the photographer didn't know was, most of the photo album at the center of the table and other pictures that filled the table were computer enhanced; made lighter or darker so to not give away the color of rock in order to hide the locations we were zooming in to hide geographical information and to enhance the exact proof. We needed to show the portrayal of each of the Peralta Stone Tablets. Mike sat down on one of the couches with the reporter and I began to show him a map and some pictures from our folder, describing how the pictures showed every marking 100 percent as on the map. I began showing the photographer the photo album, as he stood in front of the table shooting every page as I was making comments in relation to the pictures in comparison with the Peralta Stone Tablets. So here we are, giving up all of our discoveries and information and the location to the newspaper that was making us believe they were going to expose it to the public when they already knew they were not going to expose it, but instead they were going to make us look like a couple of losers that haven't found anything and were still searching for the treasure. What it boils down to is that Mike and I were ignorant to the fact that a lot of people with financial interest don't want the Lost Dutchman's Mine found and the Peralta Tablets solved along with the Peralta Treasure found. That's why it's called the Lost Dutchman's Mine and not the Found Dutchman's Mine.

Mike and I, not realizing they had no intension of exposing our discovery, continued on with our little meeting in Mike's living room. I also showed the photographer pictures of the small cave we had passed by accidentally up in the mountains; which was in the photo album. I showed him a picture. It was the horse of the Holy Faith as portrayed on one of the Peralta Stone Tablets, as well as the initials of Jacob Waltz, the Lost Dutchman, and the location where we found the alleged Adolph Ruth's skull fragment. All found at the cave. I did not think taking pictures of my photos in a photo album was a good idea, but the photographer told us there would be no problem. After collecting every bit of information they could, we started discussing the release of our findings to the public and notifying the right people to prevent a stampede. The reporter let us know that he believed we have found what we claim to have found 100 percent believable but, he said it would be up to the editor to see how much of the story we can print. Leaving it at that, the reporter told Mike and me he'd call us that evening to tell us if the story will go to print the following day. Everyone thanked each other and the reporter and the photographer went on their way. Later that evening, Mike noticed his caller I. D. was blinking. It was the reporter that had called. Mike returned his phone call. He said the story was going to print tomorrow. Mike asked him if he could proofread the article before it went to print. The reporter said it was not one of their policies. Then Mike asked him if he could have a little preview over the phone. Then the reporter said, "You and your brother are going to be the stars of a story about the treasure you claim to have found." Then he said, "If it doesn't print tomorrow, the only reason would be because something major has happened it could take up too much space."

Well tomorrow comes and no article. Mike called the reporter and asked him what happened. The reporter said, "The reason we did not make the paper was because someone got shot last night and it was possibly the work of one of the serial killers on the loose that made the front page. Then the reporter said that the editor wanted us on the front page and that is why we are waiting for another day. Now, Mike and I felt we were going to get the notoriety we worked so hard to achieve. Countless 12 hour trips into the mountains with trails of blood running down our arms; vultures circling over head smelling the blood of what they hoped could be their next meal. Face to face with a giant Diamondback rattlesnake, one of the deadliest in the country. Blue Racers were another poisonous snake that has occasionally crossed our path, not to mention the deadly heat from the sun that almost took Mike and Walter's lives. Hanging from the cliffs with rope that again almost took Walter's life. Death has been all around us from the beginning and so have the spirits in the mountain that we believe have protected us and guided us through this wild and very dangerous adventure.

It was October 27, Mike and I went to the nearest store to pick up the Mesa Tribune Newspaper. There it was on the front page. As we began to read the article, Mike and I were totally shocked by what we were reading. They seemed to be more interested in Mike's long wet stringy hair and also his health problems than our

October 27, 2006

Legendary gold stays shrouded in mystery

Lore lures treasure hunters to A.J.

By ART MARTORI
TRIBUNE

Mike Johnson slumped his big frame onto a rock formation in the foothills of the Superstition Mountains, pulled off his baseball cap and ran a hand through his long, sweaty hair.

"Wicked," he said in a thick New England accent.

Johnson and his companions took a breather Monday morning, exhausted from the 95-degree heat and the hike up the looming fortress of stone. After a few minutes, he dug a battered walking stick into the dirt and continued the ascent.

The hikers intended to press deep into the mountains in search of a fortune some say is only legend: The Lost Dutchman's gold.

The 45-year-old and his brother, Bill Johnson, 46, were lured to Apache Junction by the prospect of finding the hidden treasure of Lost Dutchman Jacob Waltz.

SEE TREASURE • PAGE A2

October 27, 2006

TORU KAWANA, TRIBUNE

STEADFAST: Mike Johnson, left, and his brother Bill, both of Apache Junction, take a break on their way toward Monument Path, where they say Lost Dutchman treasure is hidden.

October 27, 2006

TREASURE: Johnsons say they found a piece of human skull

FROM PAGE A1

They had visited the area several times when they lived in Gloucester, Mass., and in 2003 moved to Apache Junction, setting up a base of operations in a mobile home at the foot of the mountains.

Every year, countless treasure hunters make their way into the Superstition Mountains, often returning with tales of riches found — sometimes not returning at all. Despite these hopeful accounts, the treasure has never turned up. And some experts doubt it ever will.

According to Superstition Mountain Historical Society records, nearly 150 treasure hunters claimed to locate the Lost Dutchman's gold since his death in 1891. To date, no one has produced the gold.

George Johnston, president emeritus of the Superstition Mountain Historical Society, said he's seen the prospect of gold lure many a treasure hunter into the mountains. But, as far as he can tell, none of Waltz's gold has made it back down.

"The problem is, when someone says they found it, we ask for the gold," the 86-year-old Gold Canyon resident said. "Then they say, 'I don't have any yet.'"

Johnston said he's lived in the shadow of the Superstition Mountains since 1950 and he's never known anybody to turn up with the gold. He hopes it will remain undiscovered.

"To me, I think the mystery is the story," he said. "I think if someone finds it or proves where it is, it will lose some of its interest."

Mike Johnson, who said his bad knees keep him out of work, hunts treasure full time. His brother, who works in the manufacturing industry, also is a treasure hunter.

The brothers have compiled an extensive archive of their findings that includes blurry photos and newspaper articles, saved on a computer Mike Johnson salvaged from a trash bin. They said they even found proof: A fragment of what they believe to be a human skull from some unlucky character in the Lost Dutchman saga.

They turned the fragment over to the Pinal County Sheriff's Office. An official in the department said the fragment has not been identified and the case is not being investigated.

Yet the Johnsons were undeterred.

"Nobody who found what we found has lived to tell about it," Bill Johnson said. He stood perched on a cliff about two miles into the mountains, scanning the area for landmarks and other clues showing the way to the treasure.

The temperature had surged to 105 degrees by the time the Johnson brothers located a cave hidden by a paloverde tree. The ceiling of the cave was layered with soot from a campfire, and an old shovel leaned against the rock wall. But the Johnson brothers, now five hours into the trek, were subdued.

Most of the water was gone. And Mike Johnson, now pale and his breathing ragged, said he was lightheaded and worried about his heart condition.

"I take 19 pills a day," he said.

But he's not the only one who's had trouble in the mountains.

The Pinal County Sheriff's Office responds to about 120 rescue calls every year, most of them in and around the Superstition Mountains, officials said. In the past 21 days, the all-volunteer Superstition Search and Rescue has retrieved five people. Three of them were dead, and two were immobilized and near death.

Deputy Ben Cook, who coordinates efforts between the search and rescue team and the Pinal County Sheriff's Office, said it's too easy to overlook the danger of entering the Superstition Mountains. It's so strenuous that rescue volunteers first must demonstrate that they can hike three miles in one hour, while carrying a 35-pound backpack uphill.

"I think it's so close to civilization that people think it's safe out there," he said. "It's not. It's as remote and wilderness as you can get."

The Johnson brothers survived the excursion Monday, which included zigzagging across a two-mile route into the mountains and climbing nearly 2,000 feet in altitude. They made it back safely, but none the richer.

Clay Worst, a 78-year-old Apache Junction man who's sought the gold for the last 58 years, said treasure hunting takes a toll on a person. The longer the search, the harder it gets, he said.

"Sometimes, it gets to be 15 or 20 years before they realize it's not as easy as they thought," he said. "But they're having the time of their life."

Back in Mike Johnson's air-conditioned mobile home, the brothers sipped ice tea and pored through files they said prove the location of the Lost Dutchman's gold. Mike Johnson had almost recovered and said he could never make the trip if he were weighted down with the fabled riches. They just want credit for the discovery, he said, and maybe a book deal.

"I can't picture myself hauling out a big bag of gold," he said. "I'd rather go for the other part — it pays the same."

CONTACT WRITER: (480) 898-6865 or amartori@aztrib.com

discoveries we made in the mountain. All they mentioned about our discovery was that we had a bunch of blurry photos. They basically made us look like a couple of guys that don't want to work and are looking for gold in the mountains. There was a big article that went onto the next page, where it showed a picture of Mike and me. Mike was sitting down with his long stringy, sweaty hair and I was just staring off into the mountain. My friends were not surprised at all after they heard the whole situation. The following Sunday another article came out in the Tribune. The title was called "Let's Hope the Dutchman's Gold Stays Lost." It said, we learned in the Thursday Tribune that a couple of fellows from New England are the latest to claim they know exactly where it is. Then it talked about how an entire industry has evolved in the Apache Junction area ever since the Dutchman's death. The whole article was basically saying that they don't want this treasure found. Mike and I understand how they feel, and it makes sense for money reasons why it should not be found. We can't help that we were spiritually led to the treasure in the mountains, which is the Church of the Holy Faith. We've got to believe that there is a much greater reason for this than just money. We need to believe that there is a much bigger plan in the works involving our discovery.

October 30, 2006

Let's hope the Dutchman's gold stays lost

MARK J. SCARP
TRIBUNE COLUMNIST

Outside of the Gunfight at the OK Corral, Arizona's greatest Old West legend has to be of the Lost Dutchman Mine.

For many it's among the first things people who aren't from here learn about Arizona. In the pantheon of Arizona yarns, right after Wyatt Earp, Doc Holliday and the Clanton gang is the story of Jacob Waltz and his gold strike, the location of which he supposedly took with him to his death in 1891.

We learned in Thursday's Tribune that a couple of fellows from New England are the latest to claim they know exactly where it is.

Not to deny anyone a rightful fortune, but the last thing the area around the Superstition Mountains, where the gold supposedly is, needs is for someone to actually show it to everybody.

An entire industry has evolved in the Apache Junction area in the more than a century since Waltz's death. Stables rent horses and guides to let visitors trace the paths of countless prospectors who have chased the legend with what they believe is the definitive map.

Of course, prospectors need tools and gear, which is available at local outfitting stores.

And the biggest annual event is Lost Dutchman Days. Whoever portrays Waltz in the parade each year would be out of a job — or at least be booed as he passed by town residents, a stand-in for the real Waltz, rightfully vilified for not hiding his gold well enough.

Waltz was actually German, and some mistakenly believe that "Lost Dutchman" indicates that he, not his mine, was the one who was lost. To the contrary, historians recount how he came out of those mountains to tell tales about his find for 20 years. He died in Phoenix, mum to the end about the gold's exact location.

Northeastern Pinal County owes as much to the legend of the Lost Dutchman as the port town of Terneuzen, Netherlands, probably owes to the Flying Dutchman, a legendary 17th century ship from that town that was cursed to sail forever as a ghost vessel, never to reach port.

According to Radio Netherlands Television's Web site, one Terneuzen bar serves pints of Flying Dutchman Beer and has a local man who dresses up as the doomed ship's captain.

Now, unless the ship actually shows up in Terneuzen someday, the Flying Dutchman's one legend that you can bet will stay a legend.

Tribune editorial writer and columnist Mark J. Scarp can be reached at (480) 970-2351 or mscarp@aztrib.com.

These spirits in the mountains did not guide us to this place for us to just keep all of our discoveries under the carpet and pretend it never happened. If we tried to keep it a secret and make an attempt to go uncover the treasure there's too many things that could go wrong. If we are caught removing the artifacts by officials, we will go to prison for a long time. We'd never make it out of the mountains alive. Or if we did make it out of the mountains with some artifacts, to us, that would be stealing from the Church of the Holy Faith and that doesn't set right with us. That treasure belongs to some organization in the world somewhere. Mike and I were talking about how we believe Apache Junction and the state of Arizona would pull in much more revenue if they made this place a monument. To build a walkway with rails all the way up to the mountain to the Church of the Holy Faith and let the world see one of the most unbelievable treasures in the world with security all around it protecting it. We believe that people from all over the world would come to see this amazing place and then tourism would go through the roof. They just want us to sweep it under the carpet and pretend this never happened. If we're to pretend this never happened, that it was just an illusion, we probably wouldn't be able to sleep for the rest of our lives just knowing what we know.

Mike and I want to make another attempt to get this place protected. We decided to call the archaeologist from Tonto National Forest. We talked to one of the archaeologist that handled the Superstition Mountain area. He said he heard of us from the newspaper. Then we set up an appointment for Mike and me to have a meeting with him and his supervisor. It was just a few days away. So Mike and I had time to get all of our evidence together for the meeting. The whole idea for this meeting for Mike and me was to get this place protected in the mountains as soon as possible, because more and more people are starting to know of this place and that it really does exist. Without a doubt there are people right now on the mountain searching for our discovery to find the treasure themselves. Thank God it is well hidden and in a very, very dangerous place. That buys us plenty of time, but doesn't mean it couldn't be found by someone eventually. That would be devastating. So Mike and I are counting on these archaeologist to get protection. We even had a friend of ours that worked for the A.J. Newspaper as a reporter that did a couple of nice articles on Mike and me about the skull fragment. She was a very nice lady and she called the archaeologist that we were meeting with and asked him to treat us fairly and he said he would. After a couple of days, we were on our way to the meeting. When we went inside the building they treated us with respect and brought us to the meeting room and had us take a seat. The two archaeologist both showed up for our meeting. Mike and I had the photo album placed on the table in front of us. We had many photographs to show them. We opened up the photo album, one page at a time showing the comparisons of our discoveries that portrayed the Peralta Stone Tablets. The one archaeologist that was sitting closer to Mike was the one who was supposedly in charge of the Tonto National Forest, Superstition Mountain area. The archaeologist sitting beside me was his boss from Phoenix. I would like to mention their names, but its probably best if I don't. The archaeologist that was sitting next to Mike was jumping out of his seat as we began showing our photographs of our discoveries. His boss who sat beside me was quiet and still and was not saying much. You could see it in his eyes, especially the one sitting next to Mike, that what he was seeing was real. That's why he seemed a little excited as he was running around the table checking out our photographs. As his boss was quiet and still now, these two archaeologist have got to be very busy men and you would think that if they truly were not seeing anything of interest in our discovery photographs, the meeting would've lasted about five minutes. Instead the meeting went on for about two and a half hours looking over every photograph. The archaeologist next to me was quiet and didn't have too much to say. After we were done showing them the photographs, it seemed like the archaeologist next to Mike was ordered to keep his mouth shut, while his boss said "I don't see anything. I don't know what you guys are talking about." That was when Mike and I looked at each other and smiled and then walked out the door and drove away. Mike and I started talking about the one that was jumping out of his seat with excitement and it was written all over his face that what he was seeing was real. We could also tell that he felt bad because his boss was not being truthful with us and he told the reporter that he would treat us fairly. Now, Mike and I've realized that meeting with these state archaeologist was probably the biggest mistake that we could have made, because more than likely they will do anything in their power to stop this discovery from reaching the public. It made me wonder if we are writing this manuscript for nothing.

They might have lots of power but the spirits in the mountains also have a lot of power. We will have to see who's power is greater. All we can do is just keep moving forward and have a little faith that this mission gets accomplished. We were not sure in what direction we should go with our story, but we did come up with an idea. That was to go to the library and see if we could find a list of book publishing companies or literary agencies that we could send a letter to and just see if we can get some bites. Mike typed up a short powerful letter that we mailed out to a dozen literary agencies. Meanwhile, we kept writing the manuscript while we were waiting and hoping to receive news from one of the literary agencies. Within two weeks we got some responses back in the mail. A few of the responses said we were sorry but we don't believe we could sell this type of book, but other agencies might be able to. These agencies had no idea of the intensity of this story and what was involved here. We gave them no information on what it was about accept it had something to do with the Lost Dutchman's Mine in the Superstition Mountains and that we had been on the adventure of a lifetime and we couldn't live with ourselves knowing what we know. A couple more days had passed and two more responses came in the mail. They were both from Connecticut. One response said, "I'll take a look." That's all it said. And the other response said. "Thank you for your query letter regarding your nonfiction project. We read your letter with interest and would be happy to consider the project." They asked us to send them a hard copy of the full proposal, including two sample chapters, a complete outline and our C.V. It took us about two months to put the package together and mail it to the agency. After six weeks we had not heard from them. So we made a phone call and left a message saying we were assuming you're not interested and we'd appreciate it if you mailed our package back to us. Within ten minutes the phone rang. It was the agent. She said that she doesn't need to send it back to us and that it was being considered. Mike said, "Oh, I'm sorry, my brother and I assumed you were not interested since we had not heard from you in six weeks." Mike got off the phone with her. It was such a relief knowing they read the sample chapters and it was still being considered. Now we had to just wait and be patient. We continued writing the manuscript. Four months had gone by and we never heard another peep out of the agent or the agency. We tried calling them and left a message and they never called us back. But you would think if someone did stop them from considering our book, they would at least send us a letter or something saying they're no longer interested. But they did not do that and they still have our package with the photographs. If they're not interested then we will need that package returned to us or a quick, simple letter. Common sense tells us something is wrong. We realized that we couldn't dwell on this and we need to move forward. Mike and I believe that we could be in serious danger and have not forgotten that nobody has ever lived to talk about what we know.

That's why they call it the curse of the Lost Dutchman's Mine. Who is really behind what they call the curse of the Lost Dutchman's Mine? It really makes us wonder when nobody's being truthful with us. I know one thing, I'm sure having my thoughts about who could be behind the curse of the Lost Dutchman's Mine. And if what I'm thinking is right, we are in serious trouble. We've decided that if we just finish writing the manuscript, we'd have a much better chance of getting published or getting the help we need to get it done. I continued going to Cobbs Restaurant every day to work on the manuscript. The days would roll over into nights as we continue writing our manuscript. I always feel like I'm being watched. It's probably just paranoia, but because of the situation I'm probably better off assuming that I am being watched and keep my eyes open for any strange behavior. Things are starting to get really weird at Cobbs. Some girl came in that I've never seen before. She sat by herself while she was drinking coffee when all of a sudden she asked me to sit with her and I did. Then she asked me a very strange question. "Do you know why I'm here?" Then she told me something that I was not expecting. She said, "I know what you've been doing and you need to pretend it is all just an illusion." I said "What do you mean?" She said, "You know, this deal in the mountains." I was in total shock when she said that. "You need to start telling people you just imagined it." Then I got up and went to the restroom to throw cold water on my face. When I came back out about one minute later, she was gone. The next day, I went to see my brother Mike and told him about the woman and what she said to me. Mike said, "Well that's just too weird."

Now we realize that we are in more danger than we thought. We need to move away from the Apache Junction area, but neither one of us can afford it at this time. So we don't have much choice. We need to just stay put and keep moving forward and hope our manuscript makes it to the book stores nationwide. Then we will be a lot closer to the truth. The real truth lies behind the hasty wall in the center of the heart. There are too many questions. Will the spirits in the mountain allow anyone to open up the hasty wall or will the truth stay hidden?

EPILOGUE

Photo Finish

In a very high place in the Superstitions, six rectangular stones spells DON. Like the six stones on the back of the insert heart. Like the six stones on the discovery heart spells DON .Like the Peralta stone spells DON with a heart above to the right.

The stone tablet that spells DON with a heart to the upper right.

The stone tablet the cross shows who ever created the Peralta Stone Tablets was a person of faith.

The secret entrances, as you have not seen in photographs of the discovery heart. They are virtually invisible, you can't see them till your just feet away. Almost halve way up the discovery heart, if you look closely you can see what looks like waves. These waves is what you see in the picture above, slits that go sideways that lead you into the discovery heart area. The slits are angled in towards the cliff and face the sky which makes them invisible. Inside you drop 8ft down, the rest of the heart stands in front of you. Turn to your left and walk into a box canyon full of vegetation as well as mesquite trees and some of our other discoveries.

Mike's ice container has produced a picture through it's oxidation process of who we believe to be Jacob Waltz. We did not notice the picture till we had made most of our important discoveries. It was only feet away when we made our discoveries and he was watching us the whole time.

The odd shaped head in the center of the picture above is the one we believe is on Ruth's Map. It is on the Johnson Discovery Map in it's actual location. The cave on the Discovery Map is also on Ruth's Map where we believe he was murdered.

The sun shines through the eye of the needle in the direction of the discovery heart, southeast from the heart of our discoveries.

The spiritual orb appears where Bill and Mike worked in his house. The same place the silver ice chest sits on a carousel.

This carving of Jesus needs to be compared to the shroud of Jesus we believe they can authenticate each other. As your looking at this carving you can see what looks like a circle on the eye to the right with a candy cane symbol inside it. This will be important to tie these images together.

Mike was watching a documentary close to Easter on the shroud of Jesus. They were talking about the latest technology they were using to unleash it's secrets. They were using a technology called quantum physics which let them get a 3D look at the impressions left by Jesus. The most interesting part was when they found that Jesus had two Egyptian pennies that had candy cane symbols covering his eyes. If this was only discovered recently, so when and who carved this enormous portrait and how did they know about the coins?

ACKNOWLEDGMENTS

The authors wish to acknowledge the invaluable assistance of the following people:

Kathy Hall for her work as a reporter and doing two stories on the alleged Adolph Ruth skull fragment encouraging us to put our story in the paper.

The Apache Junction Newspaper for allowing Kathy Hall to write two excellent articles about the alleged Adolph Ruth skull fragment.

Tonto National Forest for lending an ear, whether they believe our story or not.

The East Valley Tribune Newspaper for printing us in the spotlight as legitimate treasure hunters.

Goldfield Ghost Town for permitting us to take photographs of the Peralta Stone Tablets while giving us a personal tour of the Mammoth Gold Mine.

The Apache Junction Historical Society for taking the time to listen to our story at a time that it may have been hard to believe because of not having all the facts to verify our story.

Linda Dutton for her help typing the manuscript and her technical help in editing the manuscript.

Mesa Southwest Museum for taking us into their laboratory and conducting a test on the alleged skull fragment of Adolph Ruth.

Debra Crest Johnson for her wholehearted support and participation in helping us prepare to take our many trips into the Superstition Mountains right up to her untimely death on July 30, 2007. Debra, we thank you Wholeheartedly and we will miss you.

BIOGRAPHY

William A Johnson born June 6, 1958 Gloucester, Massachusetts, as a child I spent most of my time pounding on pots and pans throughout the house. At the age of six I got my first drum set for Christmas. Living across from the school I spent a lot of time playing along with the High School's marching band in my own living room.

At the age of 10 years old I got a pair of hockey skates and I quickly learned the art of pond hockey with all the kids in the neighborhood. Around this same time I stated my first band. I was pursuing music and hockey until my father was approached by my coach and told I was one of the best he's seen.

I was soon sent to a hockey school being taught by several members of the St. Louis Blues, and was excelling. Then I made one of the biggest decisions of my life to that point and abandoned hockey to pursue music full-time. By the time I was 18 I had learned the keyboards and was fast becoming a singer/songwriter.

In my late 20's I became a father to a lovely daughter. I raised her alone for 17 years until I moved to Apache Junction, AZ so she could be closer to her mother. This move and my career as a songwriter help me to write A Thrilling Discovery in the Superstitions.

Michael R. Johnson born on November6, 1960 in Gloucester, Massachusetts; as a child I was known as "The Wanderer" because of my desire to travel. I had to be put on a leash because of my wanderings when I was left outside alone to play.

I found myself fascinated by elderly people and all the tales they had to tell about their experiences in life. One of my favorite people was the captain of an old clipper ship by the name of Captain walker. In going to his house I had to cross a drawbridge, which would let the boats in and out of the port. Objects and people that were very old caught my attention.

My brother William and I earned our allowance by helping clean the court-house after Sunday School where my father was a local police officer. As a treat my father would take us to Good Harbor Beach where there was an old shipwreck to search for coins or treasure. We learned much later that the coins were coming from a hole in my father's pocket; this instilled a love for treasure hunting in both of us from an early age.

We soon moved to one of the oldest houses on Wheelers Point right on the river. I found my first antiques where people used to burn their trash down by the water so the surf could extinguish the fire that had been laid in a it. My first antique sale was for old bottles that wouldn't burn and I sold them for .50 cents a piece to a friend of my father. For the next ten years I worked in many old furniture and antique stores, which furthered my interest in treasure hunting and very old antiques.

At the age of 23 I opened my own antique store. I was featured in the news-paper after doing some remodeling of my old store and finding behind the panels some very old murals depicting the Gorton Fish Factory with wagons and carts of fish and wooden barrels used to salt the fish to preserve them. Soon after another article was written in the "Gloucester Daily Times" because of another discovery behind another panel, which depicted the 1927 "The Great Race" a clipper ship race between the United States and Canada.

Years later after a major car accident that took many years of recovery, my interests turned to treasure hunting and writing about my adventures in the Superstition Mountains, which allowed me to co-author this book.